QUESTIONS TO WHICH
THE ANSWER IS "*NO!*"

QUESTIONS To Which THE ANSWER IS "NO!"

JOHN RENTOUL

First published 2012 by
Elliott and Thompson Limited
27 John Street, London WC1N 2BX
www.eandtbooks.com

ISBN: 978-1-908739-30- 8

Text © John Rentoul 2012

Jacket design: kid-ethic.com
Typesetting: Louis Mackay / www.louismackaydesign.co.uk

INTRODUCTION

hy would you write a headline in the form of a question? It might be because you want to set your readers a quiz. What is the capital of Kyrgyzstan? Yes, well, everyone knows the answer to that one. Bishkek. No, I mean, why would you want to ask, in a headline, a question to which the answer is yes or no? Such as, 'So you think you know your capitals of former Soviet republics?' Yes. I mean, no. I mean a question such as, 'Does this book tell us something important about the state of English-language journalism today?' Or, 'Is this penguin a Communist?' Why would someone want to ask that? As an aid to open-minded intellectual inquiry, perhaps. That is how you are supposed to write essays, after all. Set out the question; define the terms; answer the question. Was the Battle of Naseby the turning point in the English Civil War? That sort of thing. It is not, however, the sort of thing that crops up often as a headline in news media.

The sort of question that crops up a lot in headlines in newspapers, and especially in the *Daily Mail*, is: 'Did Marlene Dietrich plot to murder Hitler?' 'Is the Turin Shroud genuine after all?' 'Are aliens getting less camera shy?' These are not open-minded inquiries in search of the truth in all its complexity. These are suggestions that something newsworthy might have just been discovered. Yet they are phrased as questions. Why? Well, one person who conducted a nine-year research project, studying the *Daily Mail* and its editor, Paul Dacre, is

Dr Alastair Campbell, former consultant to Tony Blair:

> The *Mail* loves unanswered questions ... you know the kind of thing
> ... Are teenagers having too much sex with their laptops? Are asy-
> lum seekers eating our babies? Does too much cellulite threaten the
> Church of England? Does Tony Blair want to be Pope? Dacre loves
> question marks because they can be used to insinuate anything that
> his demented imagination dreams up as he is driven into work.[1]

It is tempting, therefore, to assume that *any* headline that ends
in a question mark can be answered by the word no. This was
the conclusion of Ian Betteridge, a technology blogger, who
gave his name to Betteridge's Law. He wrote: 'The reason why
journalists use that style of headline is that they know the story
is probably bullshit, and don't actually have the sources and
facts to back it up, but still want to run it. Which, of course, is
why it's so common in the *Daily Mail*.'[2]

Indeed, the slogan of one of the *Mail*'s columnists, Jan
Moir, is one of the all-time great Questions to Which the Answer is No: 'Are you thinking what she's thinking?' After all, if
the answer were yes, the newspaper could assert the insinua-
tion as fact. 'She's thinking what you are thinking' or 'Church
of England threatened by excess of cellulite' or 'Marlene
Dietrich plotted to murder Hitler'.

Betteridge's Law is an attractive hypothesis. Unfortunately,
having tested it in laboratory conditions – that is, by reading
things in newspapers and on the internet – I have established
that it fails to capture the full complexity of modern journalism.

For a more sophisticated analysis of the art of writing
headlines, therefore, let us turn to Alan Beattie, International

---

1. Alastair Campbell, blog, 16 October 2009.

2. Ian Betteridge, 'TechCrunch: Irresponsible journalism', Technovia blog, 23
   February 2009.

Economy Editor of the *Financial Times*. He promulgated Beattie's Immutable Law of Headlines, as follows:

> If there's a question mark in the headline the answer is either (tabloid) 'no' or (broadsheet) 'who cares?' For example: 'Is Jackson Widow Serial Killer?' No.
>
> 'Is Bordeaux the New Provence?' Who cares? 'Have The Police Gone Stark Staring Mad?' No. 'Do Women Prefer Vladimir Putin's Body to Jack Nicholson's?' Who cares?

Perhaps the finest question in the broadsheet category was one asked by the *Wall Street Journal* on 24 March 2011: 'Why have dinner napkins gotten so darn small?' As Beattie said: 'The genius of this is that it identified a trend which I haven't noticed *and* about which I wouldn't care if I had.'

Inevitably, further investigation in the laboratory found that even Beattie's Immutable Law turned out to be, well, mutable. First, a reader pointed out that it was silent on the matter of magazine headlines. Beattie acted swiftly to fill this legislative omission, returning from another trip up the mountain to hand down a Protocol to the original Law:

> For women's magazines, the answer is: 'Dunno, and your stupid quiz isn't going to tell me.' (In response to, for example, Could You Be Co-Dependent? Are You Your Own Best Friend? Is Your Cellulite Abnormal?)
>
> For men's magazines, the answer is: 'Dunno, but I'm sure you're about to tell me.' (In response to, for example, Is The Nokia N8 The Hottest Phone of 2008? Is 'Four Lions' Violent Enough? Are You Britain's Best-Dressed Man? – all genuine headlines from *GQ*.)

Just as subatomic physicists are always getting close to formulating a single theory that explains everything from quarks to supernovae, without ever quite doing so, the Immutable Law of Headlines, even with its Protocol, still falls short of the elusive ideal. We are close to a unifying theory of headlines in the form of questions, but not quite there.

There is still, for example, the problem of what might be called the 'double-bluff question'. For example, Laurie Penny of the *New Statesman* asked on 2 March 2011: 'Is it crass to compare the protests in London, Cairo and Wisconsin?' This is an inversion of the *Daily Mail* technique. Instead of suggesting that the answer to the question is yes when it is no, Penny's subeditor was suggesting that the answer was no when it was yes. Penny suggested that the common criticism of people, such as she, who drew parallels between the Arab spring and anti-government protests in the west was mistaken. The sub-headline on her article argued, 'The difference between Tahrir Square and Parliament Square is one of scale, but not of substance.' I disagree, and say that 'crass' is a good description of her view.

There is also, however, the Battle of Naseby kind of question, the earnest dispassionate inquiry where a writer poses a question of genuine public interest and seeks to answer it. Needless to say, these open questions are rare, and indeed, for some reason, the answer to them is usually no, but it can on occasion be yes, and the diligent searcher after truth has to read the thing to find out. This is a form favoured by writers as different as Gavyn Davies, the brilliant economist who was also once chairman of the BBC, and Mike Smithson, the founder of the equally useful Political Betting website. Davies often asks questions such as 'Can a banking union save the euro?' in the headline of his posts on his blog – and I assume that he writes the headlines himself, which is usual on blogs if not in newspapers. Asking a question can be a good way of setting out an argument about a technical and difficult subject. Another question he asked himself, around the same time, was: 'A parallel currency for Greece?' In both cases, his answer was no. 'I am inclined to believe that a parallel currency could only work in a parallel universe, not the one we currently inhabit,' he wrote in answer to his second question. 'But it would be very nice to be wrong about this.'

Smithson's headlines, which I assume that he too writes himself, feature in my list in these pages. This is a little unfair, because he generally uses them not to pretend that unlikely things are likely but to provoke debate among his site's large and well-informed readership. That means that the answer can be yes. Just recently, for example, he asked, 'Will the new parliamentary boundaries really make that much difference?' 'Can George Osborne go on with declining backbench support?' and 'Could the Tories split themselves once again over Europe?' The answers are, of course, yes, yes and yes. But in more cases the answer is no, and sometimes the question looks like an attempt to suggest otherwise. 'Is Blair back in the frame again for the EU job?' Smithson asked on the day the European Council met to appoint Herman Van Rompuy to the presidency. And, when the Conservative and Liberal Democrat coalition announced the tripling of tuition fees, he asked: 'Will today mark the end of unrealistic election pledges?'

This, then, is the rule for including questions in my series: it is a list of headlines in the form of questions to which the answer is no when the writer or publisher implies that the answer is yes. By writer, I mean the writer of the headline, which in a newspaper, as I have already noted, usually means a sub-editor rather than the named author. I invented several other arbitrary rules, mostly so that I could break them. One was that questions in the *Daily Express* did not count, as it was not a newspaper. In my defence, this was the period in which the *Express* frequently put confected stories about Madeleine McCann on its front page. However, as I allowed questions from blogs, including some peculiar ones with names such as abovetopsecret. com, I decided that I was being needlessly judgemental. After a while I allowed questions that were not even headlines. Still, it was my series, so I made the rules. But how did it begin?

Once upon a time

My series of Questions to Which the Answer is No started in 2009, with a bishop, a grudge against Marks & Spencer, and a two-page spread in the *Daily Mail*. I had been inspired by Oliver Kamm, my friend and hero, who wrote about 'Great Historical Questions to Which the Answer is No' on his blog. He was one of the pioneers of the web log, and one of the best. I think he first referred to these questions on 17 August 2005. He wrote that a 'writer of a letter in the *Guardian* appears to be bidding for a place in the series "Great Historical Questions to which the Answer is No"', by asking: "Henry Kissinger – isn't he the bloke responsible for the 9/11 atrocity?"'

The letter-writer's reasoning was not direct, but it was still wrong. He suggested that 9/11 was a reaction to American foreign policy over decades, including 'the US-inspired military coup that killed off the democratically elected government of Chile and installed the murderous Pinochet dictatorship'. Kamm responded:

> I have no sympathy for the atrocious Pinochet regime, hold to very different foreign-policy premises from Henry Kissinger, and find much to criticise in his record as Secretary of State. But these questions have no bearing on the myth that Kissinger was 'the bloke responsible' for the coup in Chile. No one has ever been able to demonstrate this, for the simple reason that it isn't true.

This came as a surprise to me, because the 1973 coup in Chile was one of my earliest political experiences. Around my fifteenth birthday I was so animated by the wickedness of the US in interfering to bring down the elected socialist president Salvador Allende that I went to my first protest meeting. However, Kamm is undoubtedly right and I was wrong.

Another Great Historical Question, with the same answer, was pilloried by Kamm when Peter Hitchens asked in the *Mail on Sunday* in July 2008 about the causes of bloodshed in the former Yugoslavia: 'Could it have been connected with the ruthless economic liberalisation forced on it by dogmatic Westerners at the end of the Cold War?' Kamm dealt with such nonsense briskly, wondering if Hitchens had heard of Slobodan Milosevic.

Kamm's example must have been in my mind when I came across this long sub-headline in the *Daily Mail* on 6 February 2009:

> He's the outcast bishop who denies the Holocaust – yet has been welcomed back by the Pope. But are Bishop Williamson's repugnant views the result of a festering grudge against Marks & Spencer?

Such was my youthful arrogance that – I can admit this now – I did not read the story at the time. I knew that I did not need to. Luckily, I was right. Three years later, I can confirm that it quoted Edna Andrews, the family's housekeeper, who said that Bishop Williamson's mother thought that his father, a hosiery buyer, had been denied promotion at Marks & Spencer because he was not Jewish.

My blog post described it as 'Number 91 in an occasional series of headlines in the form of a question to which the answer is no'. This was not strictly true, or even true at all. I started at 91 to give the false impression that the series had been running for some time. To add to the pretence, I suggested that the series had been going for at least five years: 'Prize exhibit of the genre', I said, remains the *Independent*'s front page headline, on 29 January 2004, on the publication of the Hutton Report on the death of David Kelly: 'Whitewash?'

I will not go into that debate here, except to note that Simon Kelner, the editor of the *Independent* at the time, told me later that he wished that he had not put a question mark on the headline. He says that, had the report been published a few weeks later, he probably would have left it out, as the *Independent* was moving towards more opinionated front pages – those of a viewspaper not a newspaper, as Tony Blair put it. As it was, the question mark hardly made a difference to how people recalled the coverage of the Hutton report. If my series demonstrates anything, it shows that asking a question is often interpreted as an assertion that the answer is yes. Blair himself wrote in his memoir: '"WHITEWASH" screamed the *Daily Mail* headline the next day.'[3] The *Daily Mail* front-page headline was actually: 'Justice?' (One of the smaller number of questions in that newspaper to which the answer really was yes.) The *Mail* used the word 'whitewash' only in its page four report, which said mildly: 'The Government's critics were describing the report as a whitewash.' Which, thanks to the *Independent*, question mark or no question mark, was true.

This was not the only time that the former Prime Minister featured in the invented history of my series. On 24 June 1998, Trevor Kavanagh, the political editor of the *Sun*, asked: 'Is this the most dangerous man in Britain?' His question referred

---

3. Tony Blair, *A Journey* (London: Hutchinson, 2010), p463.

to a picture of Blair, on account of his ambition to persuade Britain to adopt the euro. It was an odd question, because the euro could have been adopted only after a referendum – an instrument much demanded by Eurosceptics – which was why it never seemed likely that it would happen. Indeed it was a tribute to Blair's persuasive power that the *Sun* was so fearful of him.

Later, I noted other examples that pre-dated the actual series. Nicholas Carr, in the July–August 2008 issue of *The Atlantic*, asked: 'Is Google making us stupid?' This is a persistent question, asked in sundry variations that suggest that, far from opening up limitless possibilities, technological progress is dumbing us down. I passionately disagree. A similar question that often recurs is 'Will robots replace human journalists?' I passionately believe that the answer to that question is no, too.

Imagine my delight, also, when I discovered that the title of Francis Fukuyama's 1989 essay had a question mark at the end of it: 'The End of History?' It is often assumed that Fukuyama had said that history was at an end. Instead, he was up to the same game as the *Daily Mail*, of using a question as a way of implying something without actually asserting it. Mind you, in this case it was understandable that people might have thought that he had stated the end of history as a fact, because they confused him with Walter Sellar and Robert Yeatman. They said, in *1066 And All That*, published in 1930, that, as a result of the Great War, 'America was thus clearly top nation, and History came to a .' They then set a test paper called 'Up to the End of History', which includes such gems as:

4. 'An Army marches on its stomach' (Napoleon). Illustrate and examine.

5. Account (loudly) for the success of Marshal Ney as a leader of horse ...

9. Comment *Quietly* on (a) Tariff Reform. (b) Mafeking Night. (c) The Western Front ...

12. What price Glory?

Mind you, they were just as wrong about the end of History as Professor Fukuyama was.

The second T is silent

Thus was an internet meme born. Or, rather, stolen. I may have put 'meme' on the Banned List,[4] but on this occasion it is the correct word. A self-replicating idea. I thought I was just joking around on the *Independent* blog, amusing myself mostly. I came across other Questions to Which the Answer is No and commented on them. 'Can we use Twitter to break the political-nerd ghetto?' 'Is Gordon Brown insane?' 'Is this cat really psychic?' Many of them were from the *Daily Mail*, but by no means all. Then readers started to send in their own suggestions. Many of these came from Oliver Kamm, but by no means all. The series gained a life of its own. I am not, as you might have guessed, an avid reader of the *Daily Mail*, except for the purposes of knowing the enemy, but other people became proficient at spotting its headlines for me to include in the series. Having started as a thief, I became a curator. I just had to wait for the suggestions to come in, number them and list them on the *Independent* blog.

When Twitter became more popular, I needed a shorter name for the series, because 'Questions to Which the Answer is No' is 35 characters already, so I started to use the hashtag #QTWTAIN. I had once referred to it as QWAN on the blog,

---

4. *The Banned List* (London: Elliott & Thompson, 2011), and updated periodically at www.bannedlist.co.uk

which would have made more sense, but which lacked the essential silliness that was required. So QTWTAIN it was, pronounced kuh-twain. The second T is silent. Some people, like those George Bernard Shaw simplified spelling cranks, write it QTWAIN, but that is wrong.

The rules of the series are policed and enforced by a frightening, but imaginary, institution that resembles the Académie Française. Known variously as the Committee, the Politburo, the Commissariat or the Executive, it admits or refuses questions to the list with what looks to the untrained outsider like caprice. Nominations made by friends of Committee members are nodded through when it is perfectly clear that the author of the question intended the answer to be 'no' all along, while other nominations which observe the rules scrupulously are held up in working parties or task forces for months or years.

So popular has the series become that it was described by *The Economist* as a 'cult'. Actually *The Economist* said it had acquired a 'cult following', which possibly meant that it was popular among a small number of intense and rather peculiar people. The initiation rites of the cult are not well known, but it has gained adherents in at least two other countries. The French chapter is in fact run from London, by my colleague Michael McCarthy, who reads *Le Monde* and spotted this question in it: *'Des smartphones bientôt équipés d'airbags?'* Which, unless they celebrate All Fools' Day on 16 August in France, appeared to be a serious question. The German chapter of the cult, meanwhile, has been riven by disputes over the correct translation of its name. Its first question, asked by a magazine called *Stylebook*, was: *'Ist dieser Mann die schönste Marilyn?'* (Is this man the most beautiful Marilyn?) This was drawn to my attention by Jenni Thier, who said that QTWTAIN in German was FDANL, *Fragen, deren Antwort Nein lautet,* or 'Questions, the Answer is No'. Others had other ideas, but I left them to it.

After all, I had a meme to curate. (Although 'curate' as a verb is on the Banned List too.) Questions to Which the Answer is No has been an irregular feature of the *Independent* blog since February 2009. It has ignored attempts to undermine it by people asking questions such as, 'Is this a question to which the answer is no?' (asked by Martin Rosenbaum) or 'You realise if one answer turns out to be yes, you're finished?' (Rich Davidson). Ian Leslie, another friend and brilliant blogger, even asked: 'Do you ever think the Questions to Which the Answer is No joke might be getting stale?' No sooner had he asked it, however, than he realised it was a question that answered itself.

By the time this book went to press, the series had reached number 829, and an edited compilation of the best of them is reproduced here. I have kept it chronological, so I suppose you could say that it provides an eccentric view of the history of the period 2009–12. In politics it was the last year of Gordon Brown, the formation of the coalition government and its first two years. There was a lot of speculation about the outcome of the election in 2010, including one of my favourite questions, 'Could the Lib Dems win outright?' There was a royal wedding the next year, and the Arab spring, all against the background noise of the global financial crisis. Many of the headlines collected here, however, are just odd. There are some recurring themes, such as *Doctor Who*, which may reflect my interests, and the alleged persecution of Christians in coalition Britain, which may reflect those of the *Daily Mail*. As such, this book is like a child's time capsule, containing an arbitrary selection of objects that provide a distorted picture of the period. If this book were the only historical source for those three years available to an alien, or yeti, he, she or it might imagine that the British media of that time enjoyed a long 'silly season' and was forced to resort to some desperate measures to fill its pages. But there is no quiet news season now, if there ever was. I was collecting specimens for my collection all year round.

Much of the subject material might form a study subtitled, 'A Typology of Popular Irrationalism in Early 21st-Century Media'. Many of the conspiracy theories are long lasting and by no means confined to the period. Aliens, yetis, anything to do with Jesus, the murder of John F. Kennedy, the death of Marilyn Monroe and the influence of 'supermoons' (when the Moon comes closer to the Earth and appears larger in the sky): these are enduring themes of a certain sort of journalism. A few are more contemporary, such as the wilder expanses of opposition to the Iraq war, and one suggestion (the *Daily Mail* again) that the swine flu pandemic of 2009–10 was a profit-seeking venture by the drugs companies, although both draw on timeless themes of the wickedness of politicians and multi-national corporations.

Indeed, if this book had a serious purpose, it would be to make fun of conspiracy theorists, and especially of newspapers that pretend to engage in fact-based journalism. One of my favourite leading articles in the *Daily Mail* appeared in July 2010 and declared: 'The *Mail* has a healthy scepticism of conspiracy theories.' Some people complain that Paul Dacre is overpaid for what he does, but satirical writing of that quality is without price.

One of the consistent themes of conspiracy theorists, as it happens, is that they are 'just asking questions'. They are not saying that we are ruled by lizard people from the lower levels of the fourth dimension – we have a healthy scepticism of David Icke's beliefs, after all – but we just ask the question:

why is David Cameron so reluctant to condemn reptiles? As David Aaronovitch explores in his brilliant book, *Voodoo Histories: The Role of the Conspiracy Theory in Shaping Modern History,* 'just asking questions' is one of the great defences of paranoid delusions through the ages. Conspiracy theorists often pretend to be oblivious to the implication of 'just asking the question'. Thus one conspiracy theorist asked me whom I 'represented' in expressing the view that David Kelly, the Iraq weapons inspector, had committed suicide. When I objected, he said: 'I did not accuse you of representing anyone. I asked you who you represented – a very different thing. It's a question you still haven't answered.'

Fortunately, this book does not have much of a serious purpose. It is at this point that the author of a more serious work might suggest to the reader to what use he or she is expected to put it. You do not need to be told how to use it, but one of the best ways would be this: gather a group of friends in a cheap restaurant; stand on a table; read out the headlines collected here one by one and invite the company to shout the answer. Close proceedings with a rousing chorus of 'Jerusalem', in which everyone will know what to do at the end of every other line. 'And did those feet in ancient time / Walk upon England's mountains green?' And so on. Or, you could pretend to be Kirsty Wark or Jeremy Paxman introducing a *Newsnight* discussion that turns out to be rather shorter than the producer intended, if you read out a headline and a friend pretends to be the expert in the studio who replies, after a slight hesitation to think about it, 'No.'

I hope you like it.

QUESTIONS To Which THE ANSWER IS "NO!"

He's the outcast bishop who denies the Holocaust – yet has been welcomed back by the Pope. But are Bishop Williamson's repugnant views the result of a festering grudge against Marks & Spencer?

Daily Mail, **6 February 2009.** The story quoted Edna Andrews, the family's housekeeper, who said that Bishop Williamson's mother thought that his father, a hosiery buyer, had been denied promotion at Marks & Spencer because he was not Jewish. Which is why you should never read on after a headline like that: you know that the story can only be a disappointment.

IS THIS ATLANTIS?

Sun, 20 February 2009. The *Sun* reported a mysterious pattern of criss-cross lines (below) apparently shown by Google Earth on the North Atlantic ocean bed. The BBC reported a statement from Google the next day: 'What users are seeing is an artefact of the data collection process. Bathymetric (or sea floor terrain) data is often collected from boats using sonar to take measurements of the sea floor. The lines reflect the path of the boat as it gathers the data.'

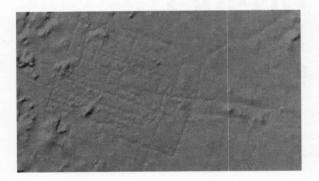

SO, IS MADONNA STILL IN LOVE WITH SEAN PENN?

Daily Mail, 28 February 2009. The online version was more heavy-handed, although this meant that it contained more explanatory material, for those of us not so familiar with the private lives of popular entertainers: 'Is Madonna still in love with Sean Penn, the man who beat her up with a baseball bat?'

Can we use Twitter to break the Political-Nerd Ghetto?

The Wardman Wire blog, 4 March 2009. Twitter was quite new then.

THE BEGINNING OF THE END?

Fraser Nelson, Coffee House blog, 26 March 2009. Several Questions to Which the Answer is No have an 'end is nigh' theme; this one referred merely to bad things happening to the economy after a Bank of England auction of Government debt failed to sell completely. Nelson thought this might mean that the Government would be unable to raise money to finance its vast deficit. Actually, it was a glitch caused by uncertainty over the pricing of gilts, as a result of the new policy of Quantitative Easing, a fancy way of saying 'printing money'.

Is Gordon Brown insane?

Janet Daley, *Telegraph* blog, 1 April 2009. An offensive and unnecessary question, I thought; the refuge of the over-expressive commentator. It was offensive and unnecessary when Matthew Parris asked it of Tony Blair, in *The Times*, on 29 March 2003: 'Are we witnessing the madness of Tony Blair?' Parris meant, 'I really, really, really do not agree with the war in Iraq.' I suppose Janet Daley's question, at the time of Brown's G20 meeting to 'rescue the world', meant, 'I am a Conservative.'

IS THE TURIN SHROUD GENUINE AFTER ALL?

Mail on Sunday, **12 April 2009.** Reported in the *Mail on Sunday* on this occasion, but repeated in all newspapers from time to time, in all good bookshops and on The History Channel. The 'after all' was a particularly deft touch, suggesting that the *Mail on Sunday* understood that any sensible person knew that the shroud was a fake, but that some new evidence had come to light that unexpectedly suggested that the fruitcakes had been right 'all along'.

National healthcare: Breeding ground for terror?

Fox News, 16 April 2009. As Barack Obama began to put his healthcare plans through Congress, his opponents held up the British National Health Service as a nightmare vision of America's future. Sarah Palin said that decisions about entitlement to treatment were made in the UK by 'death panels', and Fox News interviewed Jerry Bowyer from the *National Review*, who explained why the NHS is easily infiltrated by terrorists. Because it is a bureaucracy, apparently.

Is this an X-ray of Hitler's head?

Daniel Finkelstein at the *Times* blog, Comment Central, 20 April 2009. For this one I broke my own rule, that the author of the question had to imply that the answer was Yes for it to qualify for inclusion in the series, on the grounds that Finkelstein was asking the question on behalf of the owner of the X-ray, who had put it on eBay claiming it was of Hitler's skull.

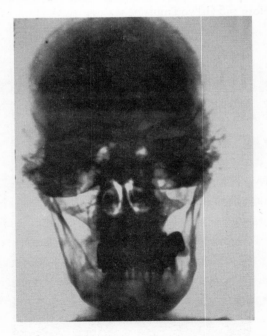

A new dawn for democracy?

Independent, **20 May 2009.** After Michael Martin, the Speaker of the House of Commons, announced his resignation, my own newspaper responded with its own brand of hyperbole, as if it were the Prague Spring and the lifting of the Labour jackboot all in one. I thought it was quite a bright day for Parliament, as it was likely to acquire a better chairperson. As for a 'new dawn', (a) we weren't exactly living in the feudal age before and (b) you must be joking.

DOES TONY BLAIR RUN ISRAEL ?

Richard Shulman, examiner.com, 26 May 2009. This was from Richard Shulman, an 'examiner' for examiner.com, 'a dynamic entertainment, news and lifestyle network'. Benjamin Netanyahu, the Israeli Prime Minister, had apparently acted on Blair's suggestion that he should hand over to the Palestinian Authority the sales tax that the Israeli government collected on its behalf. Still, it was better than the more usual question, the other way round.

Did global warming help bring down Air France flight 447?

James Delingpole, *Telegraph* blog, 5 June 2009. Again, he was not asking the question himself, as he is sceptical about human-made climate change, but on behalf of Russia Today, the English-language channel, which suggested that 'severe weather conditions' had caused the crash, off the Brazilian coast, four days earlier.

Could Lord Mandelson become Prime Minister?

Ephraim Hardcastle, *Daily Mail,* **11 June 2009.** A persistent question, first asked by Ephraim Hardcastle, the fictional *Daily Mail* diarist. Peter Mandelson was, and still is, a life peer, an appointment which, as he said, 'is for life'. Although there is no bar to a peer becoming Prime Minister, there has not been one since Lord Salisbury in 1902. The Bill that included a provision to allow life peers to renounce their peerage fell in the pre-election rush in November 2009.

Could Angelina Jolie be the first female US President?

Daily Express, **24 June 2009.** An awkward one this, because one of my early Questions to Which the Answer is No was 'Is the *Express* a newspaper?' I had formulated an arbitrary rule that its headlines did not count. But what are rules for, if not for changing?

Is Israel targeting Palestinians in Gaza by distributing libido-increasing chewing gum?

Ynetnews, 14 July 2009. 'A Hamas police spokesman in the Gaza Strip, Islam Shahwan, claimed Monday that Israeli intelligence operatives are attempting to "destroy" the young generation by distributing such materials in the coastal enclave.

'A number of suspects have been arrested. The affair was exposed when a Palestinian filed a complaint that his daughter chewed the aforementioned gum and experienced the dubious side effects. "The Israelis seek to destroy the Palestinians' social infrastructure with these products and to hurt the young generation by distributing drugs and sex stimulants," said Shahwan.'

You *could* make it up. But you would be condemned as an Islamophobic smart alec.

Will Twitter win the election for Labour?

Neil Durham, editor of *Healthcare Republic*, 18 August 2009. As I said, Twitter was still quite new.

Is the Loch Ness monster on Google Earth?

Daily Telegraph, 26 August 2009. A picture of something that actually looked like a giant squid had been spotted by a security guard as he browsed the digital planet. A similar question had been asked by the *Telegraph* six months earlier, on 19 February, about the picture below: 'Has the Loch Ness Monster emigrated to Borneo?'

Has anyone ever said something like, 'I opposed the US-led invasion of Afghanistan, I still think it was wrong, but I do recognise it made it possible for millions of Afghan girls to go to school'?

Gene, Harry's Place blog, 30 August 2009. Gene at Harry's Place was having a go at Victoria Brittain, a journalist for the *Guardian*, who was a member of the council of Respect, George Galloway's party, which is not so much anti-war as pro-war *on the other side.*

Did Diana die so that the arms trade could continue its murderous jamborees?

Mail on Sunday, **6 September 2009.** This was asked by Lauren Booth, Cherie Blair's half-sister, writing in the *Mail on Sunday*. Something to do with the Princess of Wales's campaign against land mines.

Would the left benefit from a Tory landslide?

Jonn Elledge, Liberal Conspiracy blog, 9 September 2009. As with so many of these questions, the words of Kenneth Clarke come to mind. He was intercepted by a camera crew at the 1999 Conservative Party Conference, who put Margaret Thatcher's words to him, that 'in my lifetime all our problems have come from mainland Europe'. Clarke looked disbelieving, repeated '*All* our problems?', and said: 'Well, it's a theory, isn't it?'

HAS OSAMA BIN LADEN BEEN DEAD FOR SEVEN YEARS?

Daily Mail, **11 September 2009.** Another gem of the genre, given away by the supplementary question, which was also one in my series: 'And are the US and Britain covering it up to continue war on terror?' Well, it was a theory, wasn't it?

CAN THIS MAN CURE CANCER WITH HIS BARE HANDS?

Daily Mail, **21 September 2009.** Hats off for the opening paragraph, which quoted the BBC's *Watchdog* programme as saying that this man is 'a menace', before continuing to describe how one of the newspaper's 'most cynical' reporters met this 'controversial healer' and 'her scepticism began to waver.' An example of the have-cake-and-eat-it *Mail* at its best. Rebecca Hardy scoffs at 'the most controversial healer in Britain', Adrian Pengelly, but then wonders if there might be something in anti-science superstition after all.

Is the obsession with 'climate change' turning out to be the most costly scientific blunder in history?

Christopher Booker, *The Real Global Warming Disaster*, 17 October 2009. A Question to Which the Answer is No asked, at book length, by Christopher Booker in *The Real Global Warming Disaster* (Continuum), with this question as its subtitle. I do like the quotation marks around 'climate change', just in case anyone suspected that Booker thought there was something in it.

Did Blair betray Britain for years in his bid to become EU president?

Peter Oborne, *Daily Mail*, 31 October 2009. Peter Oborne wrote that there were many times when Blair had to choose between 'doing his best for Britain', or 'creating a good impression with potential future employers in the European Union'. Only one thing wrong with this otherwise persuasive thesis. On the most famous occasion when Blair faced this choice, over Iraq, he chose to go against the policy favoured by the leaders of most of the large EU countries.

OK, so maybe we shouldn't call it the EUSSR. How about Euroslavia?

Ed West, *Telegraph* blog, 10 November 2009. This was a question that West asked in response to a sensible comment by Tim Montgomerie at Conservative Home. Montgomerie wrote:

> The 'EUSSR' thing is just one of the wholly inappropriate comparisons that often come up in debates. Other classics are Bush equals Hitler, Israel equals Nazi Germany and Britain-under-Brown equals Zimbabwe-under-Mugabe. Every comparison devalues debate and, more importantly, cheapens the suffering of the people who did live under the USSR, Nazi Germany and Robert Mugabe.

Tim Montgomerie: living proof that there are intelligent Conservatives on the internet.

Is Tony Blair about to make the most remarkable political comeback since Winston Churchill?

Adam Boulton, Sky News blog, 19 November 2009. Adam Boulton asked this question on the morning of the European Council's meeting to appoint Herman van Rompuy, former Prime Minister of Belgium, as its first President. Blair had been the bookmakers' favourite until two weeks earlier.

Boulton was not alone. Benedict Brogan wrote on his *Telegraph* blog that morning: 'Why Tony Blair should not be written off quite yet.' Mike Smithson asked at the Political Betting website: 'Is Blair back in the frame again for the EU job?' And James Forsyth on Coffee House wrote: 'Why my money is on Balkenende.'

Daily Mail, 21 November 2009. Well? Have you?

Will Tony Blair ever go on trial after the Chilcot Inquiry?

Peter McKay, *Daily Mail*, 30 November 2009. Early version of another frequent flier in this series. Far easier to ask the question, so that *Daily Mail* readers who hate Blair could fantasise about it, than to look at the law, which would be rather dull and from which any reasonable person would quickly conclude that there is no prospect of Blair, or any other politician or official, facing any kind of trial over Iraq. No matter how often I tried to explain this, and in how many different ways, the question kept recurring, with subtle differences of wording.

Does Obama have it in for Britain?

Nile Gardiner, *Daily Mail,* **9 December 2009.** The President had given a speech about Afghanistan in which he did not mention the UK.

WAS GOING TO WAR A COCK-UP OR CONSPIRACY?

Sebastian Shakespeare, *London Evening Standard,* **15 December 2009.** An unusual achievement in asking, about the invasion of Iraq, two Questions to Which the Answer is No in a single headline.

Did Darling tell Brown to go?

Iain Martin, on his blog, 7 January 2010. I said at the time that I feared that this was a Question to Which the Answer is No, and so it proved. When Alistair Darling published his memoir of his time as Gordon Brown's Chancellor, *Back from the Brink* (Atlantic Books), in 2011, he wrote: 'I met him later that afternoon, shortly after 4 o'clock … He was in a dark mood, unsurprisingly, but there was no way that he was going. He was convinced that he had to stay on and see it through. We had a long talk about the need for him to engage with his colleagues …By the time I left the room, I was satisfied that we had a mutual understanding of what we needed to do together.' A pity.

> While his wife's Lutheran Christian faith is not in doubt, is it not rather strange, in these circumstances, for an explicitly godless Foreign Secretary to send his child to an Anglican primary when there is an ordinary State school available rather closer to his home?

Mail on Sunday **leading article, 24 January 2010.** A rather special one, this, and possibly the first Question to Which the Answer is No in my collection that was not a headline. Such a pile-up of a sentence, with at least three subtextual slurs on David Miliband, that somebody must have been very proud of it.

Does the gunslinger that draws first die in real life?

Ed Yong, Not Exactly Rocket Science blog, 2 February 2010. Ed Yong reported the findings of a Birmingham University study, which found, surprise, surprise, that 'reactors' move more quickly than 'initiators', but that this is not enough to make up for the 200 milliseconds it takes to start reacting in the first place.

IS THIS CAT REALLY PSYCHIC?

Daily Mail, 6 February 2010. This cover line on the Saturday Weekend section carried a rehash of an old story about Oscar, a cat in a nursing home in America that can tell when residents are about to die.

Was the great swine flu scare whipped up by drug giants to line their pockets?

Daily Mail, 6 February 2010. A classic conspiracy theory, which would depend on executives in pharmaceutical companies taking a substantial risk of going to jail.

MISS ME YET?

A mystery billboard, somewhere in America, 10 February 2010. Spotted thirteen months after George W. Bush left the White House.

Will a hung Parliament spark a sterling crisis?

London Evening Standard, **25 February 2010.** Nor a plague of boils, darkness over the land, rain of frogs or any of the other evils predicted by a Conservative pre-election campaign against the 'Hung Parliament Party'.

Are we heading for another 1968?

Socialist Workers Party poster, 4 March 2010. This was the title of a meeting organised by the SWP on 4 March 2010, although how many of its target audience will know anything about the student unrest of 32 years earlier is debatable.

Is the Tory lead really just three points?

John Rentoul, *Independent* **blog, 11 March 2010.** Another historic first, this was a question in the series that I asked myself, on the *Independent* blog, about a YouGov opinion poll putting the Conservatives on 37 per cent and Labour on 34 per cent.

The result of the election two months later was a Conservative lead of seven points, with 37 per cent to Labour's 30 per cent, thus proving the wisdom of Tom Freeman's all-purpose news report, which I reproduce with his permission:

> A newly released statistic shows that the thing it measures has sharply and unexpectedly changed. The move takes the number index past the psychologically important level at which over-excitable fools gibber a bit.
>
> The sheer oddness of the number, which has been met with gaping and shrieks aplenty, almost certainly means that it means very little. The index usually only changes gradually, and this latest statistic represents the biggest ever change since records began not all that long ago. The nearest comparison was the sudden shift a couple of years back, after which nothing much happened except that it later turned out to have been wrong.
>
> Today's statistic is the first provisional estimate for the number covering a period of time that did actually pass some while ago without anyone noticing anything unusual. It is still liable to be revised a few times as new data comes in, then encased in concrete and dumped in the sea, before being revised again in a very quiet voice in the dead of night.
>
> A spokesman from the Institute For Stuff (IFS) said: 'You got me out of bed for this?'

Would Boudicca have been a Liberal Democrat?

Paul Richards, *Progress* magazine, 12 March 2010. This one was cheating, because Paul Richards, who asked it in an article in *Progress* magazine, did not imply that the answer was yes. He was actually making a point about the misuse of historical conjecture, comparing Douglas Carswell, the Conservative MP, who suggested that the Levellers were early Tories, to the spiritualist interviewed by the *Sun* in 1992, who was asked how Winston Churchill, Josef Stalin, Karl Marx and Chairman Mao would have voted (Churchill was for John Major; the rest for Neil Kinnock, naturally).

Do green products make us better people?

Psychological Science, **16 March 2010.** The study discussed in this article suggested that doing something virtuous in one part of your life gives you the licence to behave badly in other parts.

WAS THIS IDYLLIC FRENCH VILLAGE DRIVEN CRAZY BY LSD IN A SECRET AMERICAN MIND EXPERIMENT?

Daily Mail, **18 March 2010.** 'It seems like a crazy idea,' said Hank Albarelli, 'an investigative journalist and author' quoted by the *Mail*. 'If someone came to you and said a CIA unit were going to poison a French town with acid, you'd laugh at them. But that's what happened – no question.' No further questions, your honour. Oh, wait. There are.

Is there a sinister Labour plot to stop British troops voting in the election?

Daily Mail, 20 March 2010. At this point I began to suspect that the *Daily Mail*'s sub-editors were doing it on purpose.

VINCE CABLE FOR CHANCELLOR?

John Rentoul, *Independent* blog, 21 March 2010. This was a question asked, unfortunately, by me, on the *Independent* blog, on the assumption that Labour and the Liberal Democrats might form a coalition in a hung parliament. Even on that assumption, however, it was a stupid idea. When the Lib Dems did enter a coalition a few weeks later, the Conservatives did not feel that they had to offer them the Chancellorship.

COULD HELMAND BE THE DUBAI OF AFGHANISTAN?

UK Forces Media Ops blog, 21 March 2010. A question asked on the blog of the UK Forces Media Ops team in Helmand. If they meant did it have oil, the answer was no. If they meant would it become an environmentally unsustainable collection of air-conditioned skyscrapers in a desert, the answer was still no. If they meant would westerners there get into trouble over women and alcohol, the answer was: not for much longer.

Labour wouldn't be making us panic about al-Qa'ida ahead of an election. Would it?

George Pitcher, *Telegraph* blog, 23 March 2010. Asked by the religion editor of the *Daily Telegraph* on his blog. An update of the Government's National Security Strategy had mentioned the possibility that terrorists might try to attack London with a 'dirty' nuclear device. But this Question to Which the Answer is No ought to win some additional prize for sheer illogical noodliness. It posits this thought process in the mind of the average voter: 'I'm worried about jihadist terrorism; I was going to vote Tory but now I won't.' It makes sense to the Reverend Pitcher, anyway.

Is there now no area of our lives that the Nanny State won't poke its nose into?

Daily Mail, **25 March 2010.** The *Daily Mail* sub-editors were trying to subvert my series by making it hard to know whether they had asked a Question to Which the Answer is No or not. In fact, this, on a comment article by Stephen Glover, was not. They meant, 'Is there now *any* area of our lives ... ' Instead, they managed to ask, if you untangle the double negative and correct the grammar, 'Is there an area into which the Nanny State will poke its nose?' To which the answer is yes.

Can Twitter predict the election outcome?

Will Straw, Left Foot Forward blog, 30 March 2010. Will Straw's article had everything: microblogging, suspect use of statistics and a Question to Which the Answer is No.

Researchers say gender-bending chemicals are rife. Are they just the tip of the iceberg?

Daily Mail, 30 March 2010. The *Daily Mail* sub-editors showed increasing ingenuity in finding new ways to provoke me. 'Researchers say' is a lovely touch on this strapline, above a huge headline in the health section, 'The Toxic Timebomb'.

WILL GUAM CAPSIZE?

The Spectator, **2 April 2010.** A question asked by Alex Massie, paraphrasing a speech made in the US House of Representatives by Hank Johnson, a Democrat 'whom the good people of Georgia's Fourth Congressional District have seen fit to send to Washington', as Massie put it. Johnson was concerned that the Pacific island of Guam, an American territory, was listing and 'may tip over'.

Did Riverdance make Ireland sexiest country in Europe?

Manchester United supporters' forum, April 2010. I have no idea what this question is about, or why it was asked on a Manchester United supporters' internet forum, but I am pretty sure that the answer is no.

Will Cherie Blair sue Roman Polanski and Robert Harris?

Keep Tony For PM blog, 8 April 2010. Asked by Blair Supporter on the blog that was still called 'Keep Tony For PM' nearly three years after his departure from Downing Street, about the Blair-hating film, *The Ghost Writer*, directed by Polanski from the novel by Harris, a former friend of the Blairs'. I said she would not sue, not because the portrayal of her and her husband in the film is not defamatory, but because she is not mad.

IS TONY BLAIR A MOSSAD AGENT?

Peza, 9 April 2010. A question asked by Peza, who appeared to be a cat, on an internet forum. One reader had a good reply: 'Peza, are you drinking that vodka flavoured milk?'

Is this the most effective poster yet?

Iain Dale's Diary blog, 11 April 2010. A question asked by Iain Dale, the Conservative blogger, about this UK Independence Party election poster. The answer was, of course, no, it is offensive, silly and insulting to the intelligence of the voters. UKIP won 3.2 per cent of the vote at the election.

Is science the new rock'n'roll?

***Guardian*, 13 April 2010.** If they meant that blokes with grey pony tails would play air guitar with models of molecules and illegally download books about the Large Hadron Collider, I don't think so.

Is J. K. Rowling a secret Tory?

Toby Young in the *Daily Telegraph*, 15 April 2010. A somewhat perverse question, given that Rowling had just written a passionate pro-Labour article in the previous day's *Times*, which concluded: 'I've never voted Tory before ... and they keep on reminding me why.' She also donated £1m to the Labour Party in 2008. Nevertheless, Young suggested that she was a closet Conservative, comparing Hogwarts to Eton and Quidditch to the wall game, and claiming that Rowling's fictional school is 'heritage Britain sprinkled with fairy dust'.

Never mind that Young missed the point about the artistic imagination, he had missed an even more telling piece of evidence for his ridiculous argument. The currency of Rowling's wizarding world consists of knuts, of which 29 make a sickle, of which 17 in turn make a galleon. She is not only nostalgic for the pre-decimalisation world before 1971, therefore, but a Eurosceptic who would view a single currency divided into cents with horror.

Or, possibly, not.

This was not the end of the matter, however. Tim Johnson, a blogger known as Conservative Party Reptile, wrote to point out the following:

> The subplot of *The Order of the Phoenix* is that the Ministry of Magic is concerned that the headmaster of Hogwarts is running it as a sort of Dumbledorian madrassah, training up students to fight the Government. As a result they impose ever more centralised control of education, imposing a school inspector who gradually increases her power to remove teachers, micro-manage the school rules and eventually take control of the school curriculum itself. This process

of greater state involvement in education is portrayed as extremely malign, with the curtailment of independence stifling the quality of education and leading to a counter-productive focus on passing tests, regardless of their applicability to real life. At the end, the students rebel and force the return of Dumbledore and the end of Government meddling.

Nice try, sir.

Nick Clegg – the British Obama?

Oliver Burkeman, the *Guardian*, 20 April 2010. An early sign of the *Guardian*'s adoration of St Nicholas was Oliver Burkeman's question. Clegg had pulled off the amazing feat of exceeding the low expectations of him in the first televised debates between party leaders in British election history. The *Guardian* went on to urge its readers to vote Liberal Democrat before regretting it.

COULD THE LIB DEMS WIN OUTRIGHT?

Peter Kellner, yougov.co.uk, 20 April 2010. More Clegg-mania from Peter Kellner, the president of YouGov, the opinion polling company, with this question on his website.

HAS NOAH'S ARK BEEN FOUND ON TURKISH MOUNTAINTOP?

Fox News, 28 April 2010. Winner of the 2010 Outstanding Effort Brass Plate, asked by Fox News and first spotted, to my chagrin, by Oliver Kamm, from whom I stole the idea of the series in the first place.

Is Cherie about to go raving?

***Daily Mail*, 3 May 2010.** This headline was found on an impenetrable story by Richard Kay, a diarist, about the 10th anniversary party of Cherie Blair's legal chambers, Matrix, with added innuendo of the usual 'They're all mad' variety.

Are the BBC/ITN/Sky about to have egg on their faces?

Iain Dale's Diary blog, 6 May 2010. One of my favourites in the series, a question asked by Iain Dale on his blog on election night, shortly after the polls closed at 10pm and the exit poll, run jointly by the BBC, ITN and Sky, was published. Reassuring his fellow Conservative supporters, he wrote:

> So the exit poll shows the Tories on 307 seats, 19 short of an overall majority. Don't panic chaps and chapesses. My view is that by 4am this poll will have been shown to be wrong. It seems too incredible to be true that the LibDems are only predicted to get 59 seats. I'll run naked down Whitehall if that turns out to be true.

The result, confirmed the next day, was that the Tories had exactly 307 seats and the Liberal Democrats did not even win as many as 59 seats, ending up with 57. The naked run down Whitehall has not yet taken place.

The infertility timebomb: Are men facing rapid extinction?

Daily Mail, **10 May 2010.** A classic, asked by the *Daily Mail* and drawn to my attention by Matthew Barrett. Barrett, who started to collect a rival series of Questions to Which the Answer is No on his blog, Working Class Tory, gave up and paid me the ultimate compliment: 'You have proved to be the best compiler of useless headlines in the blogosphere.'

Will the new government reveal the truth about Iraq?

Chris Ames, iraqinquirydigest.org, 12 May 2010. A question of numbing self-absorption asked by Chris Ames of the anti-war Iraq Inquiry Digest website. The answer was of course in the negative because the old government revealed the truth about Iraq at all times. The belief that there is some hidden truth about the war that has to be 'revealed' is a conspiracy theory held by those whose opposition to the war was, or became, so fierce that they were convinced that no reasonable person could have supported it for the reasons given.

IS THIS THE MOST DANGEROUS MAN IN BRITAIN?

James Delingpole, *Telegraph* **blog, 14 May 2010.** James Delingpole, a man with possibly the most unreasonable views on climate change in a crowded field, asked this on his *Telegraph* blog after Chris Huhne's appointment as Secretary of State for Energy and Climate Change.

Are footballers rational?

Ian Leslie, Marbury blog, 17 May 2010. An easy one, this. Leslie explained why the answer is no, too, which is against the rules but the question is too interesting not to be included.

> Researchers looked at hundreds of professional penalties and fed the results into a computer, breaking them down according to where the shot was placed, where the keeper threw himself, and whether a goal was scored or not. From this they were able to work out what the optimal strategies were for taker and keeper. It turned out the best strategy for the keeper is to stay where he is. Takers send the ball down the middle about 33% of the time, and left or right about 15% each.

He did not explain what happened to the other 27 per cent of penalties, but let us not be distracted. The point is that, rationally speaking, goalkeepers ought to stand still.

> Given the high stakes involved, the hundreds of hours of experience, and the high-powered training programmes supporting them you'd think goalies would adhere to this strategy. But they don't: goalkeepers stay where they are in only about 6% of penalty kicks.

The researchers interviewed goalkeepers to find out why, and reported:

> Goalkeepers feel a pressure to act because they would feel guiltier missing a ball while staying in the centre than missing it while trying to do something.

Which is all very well but only reinforces my belief that it is demeaning for a professional sport to decide the outcome of tied matches by a bout of what is, in effect, scissors-paper-stone.

Will England become the first Western nation to criminalise Christianity?

Christian Today, **20 May 2010.** I was distracted by the constitutional novelty of the formation of a peacetime coalition government, but fortunately my friend Oliver Kamm spotted this one, asked by an Australian magazine called *Christian Today*.

COULD DIANE ABBOTT BE THIS YEAR'S 50/1 WINNER?

Mike Smithson, politicalbetting.com, 20 May 2010. The other big political story of the middle of 2010 was the start of the Labour leadership election campaign. Diane Abbott came fifth out of five candidates, the first to be eliminated, with 7 per cent of the vote on in the first round.

Scientist accused of playing God after creating artificial life by making designer microbe from scratch — but could it wipe out humanity?

Daily Mail, **21 May 2010.** A sensational return to form by the *Daily Mail* after a dull patch. This story about the claims of Craig Venter, a supposed geneticist, to have created a living cell could have been created in the *Mail*'s own journalistic test tube. Elsewhere in the newspaper, Michael Hanlon, the *Mail*'s science editor, commented on the Venter story, asking another Question to Which the Answer is No: 'Has he created a monster?'

Is David Cameron comparable to Robert Mugabe?

Samira Shackle, *New Statesman,* **21 May 2010.** This was what some Conservative MPs were saying, apparently, about the new Prime Minister's attempt to take over the 1922 Committee, which since, er, 1923 has been the exclusive preserve of back-bench MPs. David Cameron wanted it to allow ministers to attend and vote at its meetings.

An earlier Mugabe comparison had prompted me to propose a Protocol to Godwin's Law. I suggested that the following should be appended: 'The first one to compare his or her opponent to Robert Mugabe loses the argument.' Unfortunately I got Godwin's Law wrong. I thought it said that the first person to mention the Nazis loses. It actually states that, the longer an argument on an internet forum goes on, the probability that someone will mention the Nazis will approach 100 per cent. Which is sort of the same thing, expressed differently.

Have the Tories fallen victim to the Lib Dem Hug of Death?

Charlotte Gore, *Spectator*, 23 May 2010. As the Liberal Democrats got nothing out of the coalition that David Cameron did not want to do anyway, apart from a referendum on electoral reform, which they lost, and twenty-two ministerial jobs, the question answers itself.

Did Cameron tell Green to let the ball in deliberately?

Lord Soley, Lords of the Blog, 12 June 2010. Clive Soley, the Labour peer, asked on his blog if the Prime Minister ordered the England team to draw 1–1 with the United States team in the Group Stage of the World Cup in South Africa. He started his question badly: 'I'm no football expert and I'm not paranoid but ...' and blundered on: '... does anyone else think that Cameron told Robert Green to let the ball in deliberately so that the US didn't feel totally trashed and oiled up by the Brits?'

WILL FACEBOOK KILL SCHOOL REUNIONS?

Press release, 15 June 2010. This was the subject line of a piece of 'email spam', by which I think he meant a press release, received by a fellow journalist. He said the answer is 'Who cares?' (see Beattie's Law, page 7), but I said it was number 341 in my series.

Mind you, it gave me an idea. A website where you could look up people with whom you went to school and reunite old friends. Any ideas for a name?

Was the US team the victim of anti-Americanism?

Jesse Zwick, *New Republic*, 18 June 2010. Back with the football, Jesse Zwick at the *New Republic* asked another World Cup related Question to Which the Answer is No, after the Americans drew with Slovenia. Zwick wondered about the 'fateful call' in the 86th minute. Was it 'offsides', he asked? That was, of course, another one.

Is US now on slippery slope to tyranny?

Thomas Sowell, investors.com, 22 June 2010. A fine example of the genre, asked after Barack Obama had been president for nearly a year and a half. Sowell opened his diatribe with a reference to Adolf Hitler and managed to throw in Lenin's 'useful idiots' in the third paragraph. 'American democracy is being dismantled', he said, not only 'piece by piece', but 'before our very eyes', and could he just tell you what the most amazing thing is? 'Few people seem to be concerned about it.' The implication is that the heinous crime – something to do with spending public money – is being committed in broad daylight; that it is a concealed operation that no one has noticed and that takes the extraordinary percipience of the wool-free eyes of Sowell to see. Or it was possible that 'few people seem to be concerned about it' because ...

Has Wikipedia been overrun by left-wing trolls and junk historians?

Guy Walters, *Daily Telegraph*, 25 June 2010. Wikipedia is not perfect, but it is useful and is subject to no consistent bias.

IS THE NET CLOSING IN ON PRESIDENTIAL BUSINESSMAN TONY BLAIR?

Ephraim Hardcastle, *Daily Mail*, 2 July 2010. Not only a Question to Which the Answer is No, asked by Ephraim Hardcastle, the fictitious *Daily Mail* diarist, but one that used 'the net closing in', one of my favourite Blair-hating clichés from the glory years of the cash-for-honours imbroglio, the 'impeach Blair' looney tune and the anti-war 'take him to the Hague' daydream. Not only that, but the same edition featured a column by Tom Utley with a headline (one of those special long ones) that pretended the *Mail* knows what satire is: 'If Mr Blair deserves a freedom medal for invading Iraq (and banning me from smoking) then satire IS dead.' The *Daily Mail*. It's the complete package. And they can use that in their advertising if they like.

> To ask the Secretary of State for Health
> whether he plans to ban the sale of
> (a) tea and coffee with sugar and (b)
> cheddar cheese sandwiches in hospitals

Parliamentary Written Question, 7 July 2010. Asked by John Spellar, the Labour MP for Warley West, and answered in the succinct negative by Anne Milton, the minister for public health, on behalf of Andrew Lansley, the Secretary of State. The question may have been inspired by a report in the *Sunday Times* on 27 June that the Welsh Assembly had circulated guidelines to hospitals in Wales recommending 'water, juice, seeds, dried fruit, sandwiches and some low fat cakes as healthy alternatives' to sugared tea and coffee from vending machines, and suggested that cheddar cheese sandwiches should be avoided because they 'contain too much fat'.

The destruction of Pompeii – God's revenge?

Biblical Archeology Review, **8 July 2010.** Not just number 361 in my series of Questions to Which the Answer is No, but one of the all-time Great Historical Questions to Which the Answer is No. Mount Vesuvius erupted in 79 AD, 'nine years, almost to the day, after Roman legionaries destroyed God's house in Jerusalem', namely the Second Temple, in 70 AD.

Iran's new hairstyles: are they a peace-offering to the West?

Richard Spencer, *Daily Telegraph*, 9 July 2010. A question asked about a report that said: 'In an attempt to rid the country of "decadent Western cuts", Iran's culture ministry has produced a catalogue of haircuts that meet government approval.' It appeared the choice was between looking like Dustin Hoffman, Wayne Rooney with a lot of hair, or David Schwimmer.

A study is being used to support the theory many educated, middle-aged left-wingers are in fact conservatives who can't admit it. Is this true?

Jon Kelly, BBC News website, 17 July 2010. Asked in the headline on a 'magazine' feature on the BBC News website. Perish the thort, as Molesworth used to say.

Did climate change make Cameron PM?

Hopi Sen blog, 24 July 2010. Hopi Sen, one of my favourite political commentators, had this as the title of a blog post. He speculated that Labour did worse in the election because the unusually cold January and February deferred some economic activity from the first to the second quarter. If better growth figures had been published during the election campaign in April, Sen asks whether Labour would have won more votes. No.

Is the British middle class an endangered species?

Andy Beckett, *Guardian*, 24 July 2010. A gem, and the winner of the 2010 *Guardian/Daily Mail* Crossover award. The companion article, on the rampant expansion of the working and pauper classes, seems to be missing from my collection.

Do you ever think the Questions to Which the Answer is No joke might be getting stale?

Ian Leslie, communication with the author, 26 July 2010. As soon as Leslie, who wrote a brilliant book called *Born Liars* about why untruths come naturally to people, asked me this, he realised that it was a question that answered itself.

Was a Mosquito trailed by a flying saucer?

Daily Mail, **12 August 2010.** The *Daily Mail* not only asked this Question to Which the Answer is No, but provided a photomontage of what it *might have looked like*. We've supplied our own version.

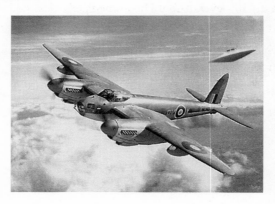

Did Churchill and Eisenhower cover up UFO encounter?

Independent, 12 August 2010. The *Independent* asked another Question to Which the Answer is No in its headline on the same story, about the release of some wartime Ministry of Defence papers. In fact, Winston Churchill did cover it up. He said: 'This event should be immediately classified since it would create mass panic amongst the general population and destroy one's belief in the Church.' But it wasn't a UFO encounter, so the answer is still no.

TONY BLAIR: BRITAIN'S SARAH PALIN?

Juli Weiner, *Vanity Fair*, 9 September 2010. This was runner-up in the Bizarre Political Comparisons category of the 2010 Questions to Which the Answer is No Awards. To be fair – a phrase horribly over-used by Tony Blair in his book – Juli Weiner was comparing the reaction to the publication of *A Journey* to that of *Going Rogue*, Palin's memoir. But the answer was still no.

Will today mark the end of unrealistic election pledges?

Mike Smithson, politicalbetting.com, 12 October 2010.
On the Political Betting website, Mike Smithson wondered
about the effect of the publication of the report by John
Browne proposing the tripling of student tuition fees. He was
referring to the pledge signed before the election by 54 of the
57 Liberal Democrat MPs, including Nick Clegg: 'I pledge
TO VOTE AGAINST ANY INCREASE IN FEES in the
next Parliament.'

USAIN BOLT: IS HE A WOMAN?

John Rentoul, *Independent* blog, 22 October 2010. I am
afraid that I asked this one, when the *Spectator* asked another
Question to Which the Answer is No: 'Are transsexuals going
to destroy women's sport?' This followed some discussion
about the case of Caster Semenya, the South African middle-
distance runner, who had been required to take a test proving her gender the year before.

WILL BARCLAYS CARRY OUT ITS THREAT TO LEAVE UK?

David Hellier, *City AM*, 28 October 2010. I think David Hellier knew the answer, but it is gratifying to look back and have it confirmed that this was a lot of wolf-crying from the financial services sector when the pitchforks were waved in their general direction.

Has Belfast film-maker found time travel evidence?

BBC Northern Ireland, 29 October 2010. Asked of a clip of *The Circus*, a Charlie Chaplin film made in 1928, in which a woman appears to be walking past while talking on a mobile phone. 'My initial reaction,' said George Clarke, who put it on YouTube, 'was that's a mobile phone, they weren't around then; my only explanation – and I'm pretty open-minded about the sci-fi element of things – it was kind of like wow that's somebody that's went back in time.' Which is the first explanation that might occur to anyone, is it not?

Zac Goldsmith: The most important politician of his generation?

James Murray, businessgreen.com, 15 November 2010. Winner of the 2010 Hyperbole Trophy. Asked by James Murray at Business Green, an environmental website. Zac Goldsmith was elected as a Conservative MP for Richmond Park and North Kingston in the election that year, and spent some of the time since threatening to resign and force a by-election if the Government went back on its pledge not to build a third runway at Heathrow airport.

HAS THE BBC GOT A GRUDGE AGAINST THE GOODIES?

Vincent Graff, *Daily Mail*, 22 November 2010. I presume this, number 437 in the series, was about the failure of the Corporation to screen more repeats. Not having read it, I am forced to speculate that Graff failed to take into account the unfunniness of the ensemble.

Can localism deliver minerals?

Mineral Products Today, **23 November 2010.** This one, from a specialist magazine, is included just for the sheer oddity of it.

Mandelson: the real PM?

BBC4, 23 November 2010. The title of Hannah Rothschild's documentary. Well, obviously he was not the real Prime Minister by then, as Labour was out of office, but the implication was that he had been while Gordon Brown nominally held the post.

Is Ed Miliband Labour's Rolf Harris in disguise?

Peter Kenyon blog, 27 November 2010. The 2010 winner in the Bizarre Political Comparison category was asked by Peter Kenyon, the indomitable Labour activist, on his blog. Something to do with Ed Miliband's 'blank sheet of paper' on which he was going to set out his policies, and Rolf Harris's catchphrase, 'Can you tell what it is yet?'

Is Wikileaks a front for the CIA or Mossad?

Richard Spencer, *Daily Telegraph*, 29 November 2010. Spencer is is a *Daily Telegraph* Middle East correspondent. I like the subtle hedging of bets: CIA, Mossad, one or the other. For the purposes of conspiracy theories, they are the same thing.

Are there any lengths to which Julian Assange will not go to slag off America and compromise the security of the West?

Iain Dale's Diary blog, 29 November 2010. This should not count, because he offered it purposely to get into my list of Questions to Which the Answer is No, but the Committee was beginning to take a flexible view by this stage.

HAS MARILYN MONROE BEEN REINCARNATED AS A SHOP ASSISTANT CALLED CHRIS?

Daily Mail, **1 December 2010.** The Committee was unanimous, one vote to nil, in declaring this to be the best Question to Which the Answer is No of the year.

79

The article quoted Phil Collins (the 'millionaire musician', in case any *Mail* readers thought it meant Tony Blair's former speechwriter), who had recently said that he fought at the Battle of the Alamo in 1836 in a former life. 'I don't want to sound like a weirdo, but I am prepared to believe.'

The main character, though, was Chris Vicens, a 26-year-old shop assistant who told the newspaper that he once lived as Marilyn Monroe. 'Yes, people have scoffed, but I know what I know,' he was quoted as saying. 'When I first awoke from my session and the therapist told me who I'd said I was, I thought: "No, that's not possible – what are the odds of that happening?"' Do not attempt to answer that question.

Chris went on: 'Each time I regress, I learn a little more. I like to think I am a sane and rational person. I am definitely not making this up. Why would I open myself up to ridicule?' Do not attempt to answer that question, either.

Is the answer to this question 'No'?

Martin Rosenbaum, Twitter, 1 December 2010. This was asked by my friend Martin Rosenbaum. I had no hesitation in declaring it the winner in that year's Smart Alec category.

Could scientists be on the verge of inventing a Dr Who-style sonic screwdriver?

Daily Mail, 6 December 2010. The Doctor's sonic screwdriver is an essential plot device, because it can open any door or lock. It also allows the Doctor to 'reverse the polarity of the neutron flow' or, in other words, to save the characters from certain doom with a bit of pseudo-scientific hocus pocus. The *Mail* reported that engineers at the University of Bristol were working on a screwdriver that could use rotating ultrasound waves to turn screws from a distance. It quoted Bruce Drinkwater, Professor of Ultrasonics, who said: 'Whilst a fully functioning time machine may still be light years away, engineers are already experimenting with ultrasonic waves to move and manipulate small objects.'

A pedant might point out that a light year is a measure of distance rather than time. For a bonus point, a pedant might point out to the *Mail* that Doctor Who does not take the contraction Dr, according to the BBC. This is something that I discovered years ago in the steam age of Google, before it had learned to search for different spellings or forms of words, when I searched for 'Dr Who' and could find little.

Did Archimedes set fire to a Roman fleet using only mirrors and the rays of the sun?

Barack Obama, *Mythbusters*, 8 December 2010. I am not quite sure why, but this was asked by Barack Obama on the Discovery Channel. For some reason the President had agreed to launch an episode of *Mythbusters*. The programme tried to recreate the legendary feat, with what success I do not know.

ARE THE 2012 OLYMPICS PART OF A PLOT TO TAKE OVER THE WORLD?

Steve Rose, *Guardian*, 8 December 2010. A top conspiracy theory from Steve Rose in the *Guardian*. The mascots (below). They're aliens. Apparently.

Is the Sustainable Communities Act the most important legislation since 2000?

Steve Shaw, Left Foot Forward blog, 20 December 2010.
I felt Shaw should really have asked if it were the most important law this millennium. But the answer is the same. I had no idea that there *was* a Sustainable Communities Act.

WILL HUMAN RIGHTS KILL CHRISTIAN ASSEMBLIES IN SCHOOLS?

Daily Mail, **28 December 2010.** It hardly counts, because it was written by a computer programmed to churn out *Daily Mail* headlines to a Question to Which the Answer is No template. But as it was the season of pretending to believe in fiction for the sake of the children, it is on the list.

Are the Queensland floods the result of Kevin Rudd speaking against Israel?

Daniel Nalliah, catchthefire.com.au, 11 January 2011. I think it was someone at the BBC who described the flooding in Australia as being 'of biblical proportions'. I should have known that there would be trouble. And so it came to pass that Daniel Nalliah, on the Catch the Fire Ministries website, asked number 483 in my series. (Biblical proportions are, of course, about 19 × 13 × 5 cm.)

DO WE HAVE AHMADINEJAD ALL WRONG?

Reza Aslan, *The Atlantic*, 13 January 2011. Asked by Reza Aslan (a cool name for Narnia fans) in *The Atlantic* with a full-form supplementary question:

> Is it possible that Iran's blustering president Mahmoud Ahmadinejad, long thought to be a leading force behind some of Iran's most hard-line and repressive policies, is actually a reformer whose attempts to liberalise, secularise, and even 'Persianise' Iran have been repeatedly stymied by the country's more conservative factions?

In fact, the article made the serious point that the WikiLeaks leaks suggested that Ahmadinejad may be less of a tub-thumping fundamentalist in private, and that there are even more dangerous elements of the Iranian ruling theocracy than he. But the answer was still no.

Is organic donkey milk the next big thing?

Soil Association, 18 January 2011. Asked by the Soil Association, which promotes organic farming. According to a *Guardian* report the previous day, donkey milk, which was 'widely sold in the UK until the end of the 19th century', contains more protein and less fat than cow's milk.

Does the death of 200 cows in Wisconsin confirm biblical prophecy?

Time **magazine, 18 January 2011.** This was drawn to my attention by Will Cookson, who had just started his own collection of 'Theological Questions to Which the Answer is No'.

Is the world's largest super-volcano set to erupt for the first time in 600,000 years, wiping out two-thirds of the US?

Daily Mail, 25 January 2011. You must admire the precision with which the *Mail* estimates the proportion of the United States that will be wiped out by an event a bit like one that may or may not have happened more than half a million years ago. With a special 'How Journalism Works' award for the use of 'set to'.

Do any of us understand the modern world?

Policy Exchange, 31 January 2011. The title of a seminar at Policy Exchange, the right-of-centre think tank, addressed by Jim O'Neill, Chairman of Goldman Sachs Asset Management. I do not think it was a lecture on the semiotics of The Jam's 1977 single.

WAS MONA LISA A MAN?

***Daily Mail*, 3 February 2011.** The article elaborated, by asking: 'Was da Vinci's young male apprentice the model for that famous enigmatic smile?'

Can complexity theory explain Egypt's crisis?

***New Scientist*, 3 February 2011.** This was the first of a mini-series of Unexpected Historical Questions about the Egypt Crisis prompted by the unrest in Tahrir Square that eventually toppled Hosni Mubarak's government. The *New Scientist* reported a warning from scientists studying complex systems, who said that 'ever-tighter coupling among the world's finance, energy and food systems' would result in 'waves of political instability,' and that 'Some say that is now happening in the Middle East.'

Alan Beattie (originator of Beattie's Law) wrote to me to say: 'Today's events in Egypt surely show the folly of adopting sedentary agriculture in the Nile valley in the 8th millennium BC.'

IS OBAMA ALREADY A WAR CRIMINAL?

Devon DB, Global Research, 9 February 2011. The 2011 winner in the Loopy But A Bit Slow Anti-War category was Devon DB, at an outfit called Global Research. By the time he or she asked it, Barack Obama had been President for more than two years, and had therefore been a war criminal by definition for all that time – long enough for even the dimmest conspiracy theorist to notice.

Will royal wedding put people in an AV mood?

Jim Pickard, *Financial Times*, 11 February 2011. A question paraphrasing the argument of the Yes campaign in the referendum on the Alternative Vote: 'Around the wedding it will be a coming-into-summer, more optimistic, more of a yes mood.' That insight into popular psychology ('Hurrah for the happy couple; let's tear up centuries of constitutional tradition') was almost faultless.

Is it time to give this disloyal, pro-Europe old bruiser the boot?

Tim Montgomerie, *Daily Mail*, 12 February 2011. Asked by the otherwise sensible Tim Montgomerie in an article about Kenneth Clarke, the Justice Secretary, in an article in the *Daily Mail*.

IS THIS THE MONSTER OF LAKE WINDERMERE?

***Mirror*, 19 February 2011.** Not the *Mail* this time, but the *Mirror*. Bonus marks to Dr Ian Winfield, a lake ecologist at the University of Lancaster, who was quoted as saying: 'It's possible that it's a catfish from Eastern Europe.' Right. The lesser four-humped catfish of Wytrzyszczka, probably.

Is Cameron leading us to a Big Society gay wedding in Westminster Abbey?

Norman Tebbit, *Telegraph* blog, 21 February 2011. Asked by the unlikely blogger and Thatcherite former cabinet minister, on his *Telegraph* blog. Although this should perhaps belong to a new series of Questions to Which the Answer is No But We Wish it Were Yes.

Can your dreams predict the future?

***Daily Mail*, 26 February 2011.** The *Daily Mail* was reporting the publication of a book by Richard Wiseman, Professor of Psychology at the University of Hertfordshire. A clue to the answer lies in the full title of Professor Wiseman's book, from which the two-page spread was extracted: *Paranormality: Why We See What Isn't There*.

Is David Cameron eclipsing Barack Obama as a world leader?

Nile Gardiner, *Daily Telegraph*, **1 March 2011.** The Prime Minister, along with President Sarkozy of France, had said some muscular things about the uprising of the Libyan people, while the US President emphasised how different he was from George W. Bush by hanging around at the back.

DID CHINA OR JIHADISTS TRY TO BANKRUPT AMERICA?

Daily Mail, **2 March 2011.** This is known in the trade as Keeping Your Options Open. The headline ran on: 'Pentagon report reveals financial terrorists may have triggered economic crash.' Which deploys another gambit known as Hedging Your Bets, 'may have' being the historical equivalent of 'set to'.

Did 'Mummy's Curse' kill Egyptian looters?

Salem News, 7 March 2011. After the democratic revolt in Egypt turned bloody, *Salem News* ('Serving Oregon & The Pacific Northwest') asked the important question. Complete with picture of Howard Carter looking at Tutankhamen's sarcophagus, taken from an internet article headlined 'Was there really a curse on King Tutankhamen's tomb?' which is another Question to Which the Answer is No.

Have MP3s killed the art of whistling?

Sophie Van Brugen, BBC News report, 10 March 2011.
Sophie Van Brugen interviewed World Champion whistler David Morris, who thought his skill was a dying art and blamed the 'personal music player'.

Is the Japanese earthquake the latest natural disaster to have been caused by a 'supermoon'?

***Daily Mail*, 11 March 2011.** Asked by the *Daily Mail* on the day of the most powerful earthquake to have hit Japan in modern times. 'Supermoon', the *Mail* admitted, was a word made up by Richard Nolle, an astrologer, to describe a lunar perigee, when the Moon comes closest to the Earth. This was not due until 19 March, nor was it explained how it might trigger earthquakes.

LIBYA: EUROPE'S VIETNAM?

Anthony Tucker-Jones, *Channel 4 News,* **19 March 2011.** There were a lot of similar questions asked, with similar answers, about Iraq and Afghanistan. Indeed, there was a book published in 2006 by Robert Brigham entitled, *Is Iraq Another Vietnam?* The questions asked about Afghanistan were more along the lines of, 'Is Afghanistan Britain's Afghanistan 1842', or 'Is Afghanistan America's Russian Afghanistan 1979–89'?

Was the world's favourite polar bear, Knut, killed by fame?

Daily Mail, **21 March 2011.** He was a wild animal kept in a cage in the wrong climate.

Was all alien life sucked into a black hole after 'white dwarf hypernova' star explosion ... and could it wipe us out too?

Daily Mail, 23 March 2011. It was at this point that I thought someone at the *Daily Mail* had finally twigged. They knew what I was up to and had started doing it on purpose. With this, they managed to ask two Questions to Which the Answer is No in one, winning the Double Idiocy Special Effort Merit Star. And, no, the use of the word 'could' doesn't make a difference.

IS JOHN RENTOUL A CLOSET TORY?

Daniel Hannan, *Telegraph* blog, 24 March 2011. Conservative Euro-MP Daniel Hannan asked this on his *Telegraph* blog. I had better not dwell on why he asked that particular question, but he presumably needed a Question to Which the Answer was No as a headline for a post in which he kindly said that the series was 'brilliant'. He was especially taken by the 'white dwarf supernova' Question to Which the Answer is No (see above).

Could your saucepans bring on the menopause?

Daily Mail, 24 March 2011. As I said, someone at Northcliffe House had rumbled me. But was that going to stop me? That was another Question to Which the Answer is No.

Is this Bigfoot?

Daily Mail, **24 March 2011**. Another hardy staple of the genre. The Loch Ness monster. A yeti. Aliens. A grainy photograph. Or, in this case, a 'new video', of an 'ape man'. And a question. Only two months later, on 28 May, the *Mail* asked of some different footage, 'Is this Bigfoot caught on video?' Surely it should have been 'Is *this* Bigfoot caught on video?' Or, 'No, really, is it really Bigfoot this time?' But the answer is always the same.

Does anyone else miss Gordon?

Craig, 26 March 2011. Another picture special. That is Craig, with John Woodcock MP on the TUC 'March for the Alternative' in London. The next question in my series was asked by Ruth Barnett, a reporter for Sky News: 'Will the march worry ministers?' As she concluded: 'On the whole, probably not.'

Are Prince's nuptials being used as cover for a crackdown on dissent?

Independent, 29 March 2011. With a month to go to the royal wedding, I am afraid that the *Independent* asked this on its front page. So the Home Secretary had a meeting with the Metropolitan Police Commissioner and the Queen's private secretary and said, 'Now, we need to put some of these Trot hotheads in jail because, er, let us come back to that. Anyway, Sir Robin, do you think it would be possible to arrange for one of those Princes to get married so that the scraggies in Che T-shirts are tempted out onto the streets and the police would have an excuse to thump a few of them?'

Is France on the brink of a violent civil war?

Big Peace website, 30 March 2011. I cannot remember now what brought this on, if I ever knew. They had not even been burning (many) cars in the *banlieus* that week.

ARE OUR JUDGES ON DRUGS?

***Sun*, 30 March 2011.** Not strictly one for my series, as it may
have been a rhetorical question, but a good *Sun* front page all
the same.

Do you have a poltergeist?

***Sun*, 30 March 2011.** The same edition of the *Sun* included this question, posed (along with an invitation to call the news desk) at the end of an article, complete with pictures and (online) a video, headlined: 'Poltergeist wrecks house in Coventry ... and kills the dog.' Shame about the dog.

IS OSAMA BIN LADEN IN CHICAGO?

***Huffington Post*, 31 March 2011.** We enjoy the extra schadenfreude of hindsight with this one, but might feel a twinge of retrospective sympathy for journalists closing their eyes, spinning the globe and ... Guess again, *HuffPo*.

ARE US GOVERNMENT MICROWAVE MIND-CONTROL TESTS CAUSING TV PRESENTERS' BRAINS TO MELT DOWN?

Mail **Online, 2 April 2011.** Although the *Mail* was now doing it on purpose, it lacked the conviction to put this in the hard copy edition of the newspaper, although the print headline, 'So what made four television hosts suddenly talk gibberish?', was a minor masterpiece in its own right.

Ballet is dying, warns Sadler's Wells chief

Independent, 4 April 2011. What do you mean, it is not a question? Of course it is, thinly disguised. Allow me to translate: 'Should ballet be subsidised if no one wants to go?'

IS THIS THE WORLD'S FIRST GAY CAVEMAN?

Mail Online, 6 April 2011. This series is all for celebrating equal rights for all lesbian, gay, transsexual and transgendered people, and indeed for people living in holes in the ground. But the people of the Corded Ware culture of 2900–2400 BC did not live in caves.

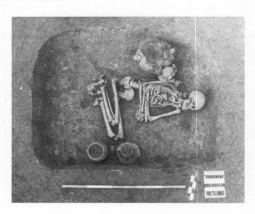

IS THE FINANCIAL SECTOR BAD FOR BRITAIN?

Liberal Conspiracy, 12 April 2011. Asked by left-wing blog Liberal Conspiracy (no, I do not know why it is called that). You can see what they were getting at, but let us get rid of it and find out, shall we?

Has an epidemic of narcissism made women delusional?

Independent, **14 April 2011.** This was the headline on an article by Charlotte Raven. The gist appeared to be that middle-aged women writing books about finding themselves had become big but rather predictable business.

Is Sunday School the root of all evil?

Andrew Lowry, *Telegraph* **film blog, 15 April 2011.** Something to do with religious themes in horror movies. The *Telegraph* seemed to have realised what the *Daily Mail* was up to, and was determined to manufacture its own Questions to Which the Answer is No solely for the purpose of getting them into my series. I refused to be put off.

Should Zsa Zsa Gabor become a new mom at age 94?

Hanh Nguyenm, *TV Guide,* **15 April 2011.** Gabor's daughter, aged 64, was quoted as saying, 'That's just weird.' Which is what usurped children always say.

Doctor Who – a threat to the political and social order?

Jonathan Jones, the *Guardian*, 16 April 2011. Another Who-related question, asked by Jonathan Jones in the *Guardian*. China's government administrator of radio and television had warned that time travel drama was 'frivolous' in its approach to history, it had just been reported. Doctor Who? Frivolous? What planet is he or she on?

BOOKS, THE NEW PROZAC?

Jeannie Vanasco, *The New Yorker*, 16 April 2011. Or it may have been, 'Prozac, the old books?'

Did Marlene Dietrich plot to murder Hitler?

Daily Mail, 16 April 2011. Now that the *Daily Mail* had professionalised its operation, this contribution was as fine an example of the genre as one could hope to see. A worthy winner in the Nazi History Reader category.

Is sugar toxic?

New York Times, **18 April 2011.** One of two fine examples in the *New York Times* on that day, the other being: 'Is sitting a lethal activity?' In both cases, we know what the newspaper is getting at, but the exaggeration is annoying. Anyway, sitting is not an activity.

Was JFK killed because of his interest in aliens?

Daily Mail, **19 April 2011.** Every time I was tempted to call a halt to the series, or at least a pause, the *Daily Mail* would come up with a corker that could not be ignored. In this case, it included the sub-headline: 'Secret memo shows president demanded UFO files 10 days before death.' A worthy winner of the Two-In-One Conspiracy Theory Award.

Does it matter what David Cameron wears to the royal wedding?

Conservative Home blog, 20 April 2011. A Question to Which the Answer was, 'Is Someone Getting Married?' There had been a flurry after it was reported that the Prime Minister would wear a tailcoat, until a hasty decision was taken by someone with a degree in the sign language of the British class system that it would be a lounge suit after all.

The G-20 Indicative Guidelines: A new improved chapter of international economic policy coordination?

Peterson Institute for International Economics, 20 April 2011. Despite the valiant attempt to liven up the question with the cliché 'new improved', it was given the accolade of the Dullest Question to Which the Answer is No of 2011.

DID ALIENS ESTABLISH A PRIMITIVE POSTCODE SYSTEM IN ANCIENT BRITAIN?

Matt Parker, the *Guardian* Science blog, 21 April 2011.
Unfortunately, the Committee, sitting in emergency session, ruled this out of order as close inspection revealed that the author had answered his own question in the negative: apparently, claiming alien involvement 'cheapens the genuine wonders of archaeology'.

Will the royal wedding break the internet?

GigaOM, 24 April 2011. A question asked by GigaOM, whatever that is, five days before the big day, which combined all the elements of idiocy for which this series is renowned.

At present, the UK uses the 'first past the post' system to elect MPs to the House of Commons. Should the 'alternative vote' system be used instead?

HM Government referendum, 5 May 2011. Number 605, asked, as part of the deal that made the coalition, by David Cameron and Nick Clegg, and answered in the negative by 68 per cent of British voters.

IS TV TOO GAY?

Fox 26 News in Houston, Texas, 5 May 2011. Fox TV was concerned about the appearance of two gay high-school couples in the latest instalment of *Glee*.

Are Cameron and Clegg cracking up?

***Daily Mail*, 11 May 2011.** By now, the *Daily Mail* seemed to be devoted to parodies designed to trick me into adding its headlines to my series. This, on the first anniversary of the coalition, was also written entirely in clichés. It opened with, 'A year can be an incredibly long time in politics,' and went on: 'Eyelids would scarcely have batted.' What kind of complexion did Nick Clegg now have? 'Pasty.' What kind of talk had he given his MPs the night before? 'A pep talk.' And its outstanding achievement was to quote not just 'a body language expert' but 'a health and well-being expert' as well. A fine day's work.

Is David Cameron such a blindingly brilliant, gorgeous, lovely, magnificent, visionary, fragrant Prime Minister that he makes Winston Churchill and Margaret Thatcher look like invisible cockroach pigmies of so little consequence I can't even begin to find a metaphor for their utter relative inconsequentiality when compared with this mighty Corialanus-meets-Julius-Caesar colossus of superlative magnificence?

James Delingpole, *Telegraph* blog, 15 May 2011. This is not a proper Question to Which the Answer is No, obviously, but it is unusual, so the Committee allowed a dispensation. It is James Delingpole's parody, on the *Telegraph* blog, of Peter Oborne's column in the *Sunday Telegraph* the previous day. Always fun when right-wingers fall out.

Did a gluten-free diet make Novak Djokovic the best tennis player in the world?

thescore.com, 18 May 2011. I do not normally do sport, apart from American football. I have a particular aversion to tennis, until they abolish the babyish second-service rule ('Oh dear, you missed, why not have another go?'). And I have never heard of Novak Djokovic. But this, asked by Irish website The Score, is a fine Question to Which the Answer is No.

Will this wind be so mighty as to lay low the mountains of the earth?

Harold Camping, 21 May 2011. That was when the American doomsday cultist predicted the world would end. All right, he did not use those exact words. Those words were used by Peter Cook in a sketch called 'The End of the World', from *Beyond the Fringe* in 1962. The answer, however, was the same.

Is this a squadron of UFOs flying over California?

Daily Mail, 31 May 2011. The *Daily Mail* did it again. Someone had left the autostorybot on overnight. The photograph might be of a Petri dish for all I know.

WERE THE SMURFS NAZIS?

Tim Karan, newser.com, 3 June 2011. The Smurfs were socialists and 'the embodiment of a totalitarian utopia, steeped in Stalinism and Nazism,' said Antoine Buéno, a French sociologist, in a new book, *Le Petit Livre Bleu*, prompting Tim Karan at the news website Newser to ask this question. Coincidentally, the BBC then asked on 27 June, possibly in relation to the film, *The Smurfs*, which was about to be released: 'Do Smurfs provide a model for a good society?' To which the answer was also no.

Is this a secret space station on Mars?

Mail **Online, 5 June 2011.** I knew my lost key would turn up.

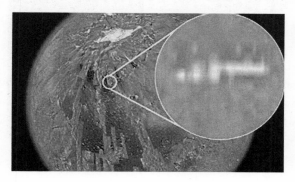

COULD LONDON DECLARE INDEPENDENCE AND LEAVE UK?

Andrew Cryan, BBC News website, 5 June 2011. Another one who thinks he can avoid inclusion in the series by using the word 'could'. No, London could not.

Is David Cameron the most Europhile Prime Minister since Edward Heath?

Peter Oborne, the *Sunday Telegraph*, 5 June 2011. Oborne thought that Cameron was more pro-European than Harold Wilson, James Callaghan, Tony Blair and Gordon Brown. Right-oh.

The end of consumerism?

Guardian, **14 June 2011**. This headline on Leo Hickman's article in the *Guardian* was runner-up for the *Guardian*-Compass Wistful Non-Materialist Trophy. The trophy takes the form of a model yurt made of goat poo.

Is Veganism the ideological glue to bring together movements for social change?

Speakers Forum session, Glastonbury, 23 June 2011. The title of a talk, away from the music, at the 2011 Glastonbury Festival. The kind of tofu-based dottiness that almost makes one want to give it all up and live in a yurt made of goat poo.

Brian Haw: A hero for our times?

Guardian, **21 June 2011.** The strange ideological alliance of the *Guardian* and the *Daily Mail* greeted the death of Brian Haw, the protester who camped in Parliament Square, with unjustified reverence on 21 June 2011.

Are 'close friends' Harry and Pippa on the verge of becoming an item?

Daily Mail, **22 June 2011.** Dramatis personae: Harry, a prince and younger brother to the heir to the throne; Pippa Middleton, younger sister to the wife of the heir to the throne. Synopsis: They had been photographed talking to and smiling at each other.

Should we clone Neanderthals?

Andrew Brown, *Guardian*, 23 June 2011. Good thing it does not arise, really.

Want a chance to win a copy of Jeffrey Archer's newest novel?

Jeffrey Archer, Twitter, 23 June 2011. A question asked by Jeffrey Archer himself, or at least by his Twitter account.

ARE ALIENS GETTING LESS CAMERA SHY?

***Daily Mail*, 27 June 2011.** The Automatic Question to Which the Answer is No Generator at the *Daily Mail* had been left on overnight again. The newspaper reported that a video 'has emerged' apparently depicting 'a mother ship and its fleet' in the sky 'above a BBC building in West London.' Extra marks for that wonderfully unspecific 'has emerged'. From the bowels of the Earth, no doubt.

Is your shampoo making you fat?

Daily Mail, 30 June 2011. For some reason the same headline appeared in the *Daily Mail* twice two weeks apart, on 30 June and 15 July 2011. Paul Dacre, the editor, was obviously trying to put me off. Would he succeed? That was question number 675.

Will Greece destroy Europe?

Prospect magazine, July 2011. This question, asked on the cover of the July 2011 edition, shows that serious intellectual magazines can be just as hysterically catastrophist as any newspaper. It did not mean 'Europe', or even 'the European Union', but 'the euro', and, even then, the answer was still no, as it was the euro that was imposing economic hardship on Greece, rather than the other way round.

IS GOD SPEAKING TO US THROUGH OUR WILD WEATHER?

Ruth Gledhill, *The Times*, 2 July 2011. Depending on whether or not one thinks He is saying, 'Thou shalt not play cricket.'

Is this the best of British?

***Daily Telegraph*, 7 July 2011.** Asked by the *Daily Telegraph* of McCain Potato Smiley Faces. Other candidates, all nominated by MPs (Smiley Faces are made in Gavin Williamson's South Staffordshire constituency), included the Aga, custard creams and loo roll.

IS THIS PENGUIN A COMMUNIST?

The Economist, 7 July 2011. I had no idea what *The Economist* was on about. Something about the threat of a trade ban being lifted on Pororo, 'one of South Korea's most popular cultural exports', which might have fallen foul of a US embargo on North Korean products, because animators from the communist North had worked on some episodes of the TV programme.

Could a wristband be the answer to dieters' prayers?

Daily Mail, 17 July 2011. Unfortunately, the question was ruled out of order. As Omer Lev pointed out, the answer could be yes, if the dieters had been praying for a wristband.

IS ED MILIBAND THE NEW CLEM ATTLEE?

Francis Beckett, Dale & Co. blog, 27 July 2011. Asked by Francis Beckett, a great admirer of Attlee. But even if you are not an admirer of Attlee, the answer is still no.

Des smartphones bientôt équipés d'airbags?

Le Monde, **16 August 2011.** The series went international with this, in *Le Monde* ('Will smartphones soon be equipped with airbags?'). Michael McCarthy, my colleague who saw this, asked, 'Is there no end to the onward march of Franglais?' Which was, of course, another one.

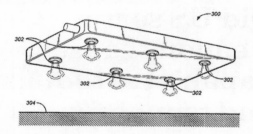

Could London lose the Olympics?

The New Yorker, **16 August 2011.** Asked by David Holmes after the previous weeks' riots, complete with a list of Games that had been cancelled because of world wars. Typical American overreaction.

IS THE COMMUNIST PARTY OF CHINA BEHIND THE TEA PARTY?

Bloomberg, 17 August 2011. Bloomberg, the financial news service, asked this about the insurgent right-wing populist movement that destabilised the Republican Party. You know, if I were an evil mastermind in Beijing, bent on the destruction of the US, that is how I would go about it too.

Did US secret weapons cause Japan's earthquake and tsunami?

dailycensored.com, 27 August 2011. Asked by The Daily Censored, a website with the slogan, 'Underreported News and Commentary'. News can be either censored or under-reported but not, I submit, both. Either way, however, the answer was no.

CAN BRITAIN EVER LEARN TO LOVE EUROPE?

Andrew Hawkins, *Total Politics*, 27 August 2011. Asked by Andrew Hawkins, chairman of ComRes, the opinion polling company, writing for *Total Politics*. The crisis of the eurozone had driven Eurosceptic opinions in Britain to new high levels.

WOULD JESUS WEAR RELAXED FIT JEANS?

Michael K. Reynolds, 30 August 2011. Asked by Michael K. Reynolds, whose slogan is, 'Real Life. Real God,' on his own website. Unfortunately, this introduced a meditation on the metaphor of using loose clothing to conceal weight gain, rather than any interesting archaeological speculation about Judaean dress norms in the 1st century.

Is this Britain's worst family?

Daily Mail, 1 September 2011. One of my correspondents, Graham, spotted this headline in the *Daily Mail*, which went on to say that the police had found a four-year-old girl, 'left home alone by her holidaying mother after arresting 16-year-old brother in stolen car.' He thought this sounded familiar, so he searched for the phrase, and found this, from the *Daily Mail* on 10 July 2008: 'Is this Britain's worst family? Head of clan with 250 convictions stole sister's identity to net £85,000 in benefits.' As he said, one of them has to be number 704 in the series.

Meanwhile a Google search for 'is this Britain's worst' found *Daily Mail* headlines for GP, drunk driver, sheepdog, holiday home, natural disaster and Christmas tree.

Could the euro crisis tip Europe into warfare?

History Today, 16 September 2011. Some of these more learned journals think that they can escape inclusion in the series by using the word 'could'. Well, the inability of eurozone countries to adjust their exchange rates 'could' contribute to a collapse of confidence in money and the end of all credit and exchange and starving gangs roaming the countryside ... No.

Is an alien invasion imminent?

PC Magazine, **19 September 2011.** The summer had seen a 'spike' in UFO sightings in America, known in UFO spotter circles as a 'flap'. *PC Magazine* suggested two possible explanations: (a) 'people are outdoors more in the summer', or (b) 'an actual alien invasion'. Take your pick.

HAS WESTERN CAPITALISM FAILED?

BBC News website, 24 September 2011. The BBC, financed by a tax on the sale of consumer goods, asked number 711 in my series.

Could cycling become the UK's second-favourite sport?

BBC News website, 26 September 2011. A diamond, asked by the BBC, which reported that, although football remains the UK's favourite sport, recent cycling success 'raises the question of whether cycling could overtake the likes of rugby, cricket and tennis to claim the silver medal in the British public's affections.' A special tin medal for 'the likes of'.

Can people spontaneously combust?

Daily Mail, 30 September 2011. An Irish coroner had just recorded a verdict of 'spontaneous human combustion', so the *Mail* asked Peter Hough, who had written a book on the subject, for his view:

> While many may scoff at the idea that the human body can catch fire and burn of its own accord, I'm rather more open minded than most when it comes to cases such as this. For, having written a book on the controversial subject and researched the area for 20 years, I have learned of many similar deaths that are very hard to explain away.

Hough's argument seemed to be, therefore: Let us assume that one of the least likely explanations is correct.

Will the e-book kill the footnote?

New York Times, 7 October 2011. Do I need to explain that a footnote is not a position on a printed page, it is a parenthetical state of mind? Oh. That is another Question to Which the Answer is No.

Is time up for Doctor Who?

Observer, **9 October 2011**. Marks were deducted by the judging panel for the rather predictable 'time' wordplay. Russell T. Davies, the genius behind the regeneration of the series, had blown himself out, it was true. But the great Steven Moffat had taken over with Matt Smith as the Doctor, and they made it come to life all over again.

IS THIS FINALLY PROOF THE YETI EXISTS?

Daily Mail, **11 October 2011**. The paper reported that the Abominable Snowman was 'close to being caught' – apparently, 'coarse hair' had been discovered in a 'remote Russian cave'. Coarse hair? What else could it be?

Does the demise of Steve Jobs spell the end of the West?

kashmirwatch.com, 22 November 2011. This question was asked by KashmirWatch, the 'Europe-based news portal of Kashmir International Research Centre' the aim of which 'is to provide news, views and opinions with background information on Kashmir'. And the founder of Apple and western civilisation? 'KashmirWatch also covers world-wide issues that impact on global peace.'

Is this an alien spacecraft parked next to Mercury?

Daily Mail, **8 December 2011.** No, it looks like a big circle that someone has drawn on the picture.

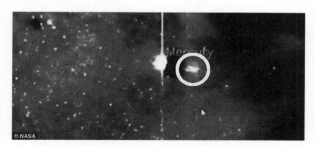

Could a group of like-minded citizens running for election for one term only, bring about the change career politicians can't (or won't)?

Andreas Whittam Smith, OurKingdom website, 14 December 2011. Andreas Whittam Smith, founder of the *Independent*, is a hero of mine. But he has some daft ideas, and this was one of them.

Was 2011 the most eventful year yet?

BBC News website, 19 December 2011. Genius question asked by the BBC, on the front page of its news website, linking to a feature with another headline of sublime comedy: '2011: The year when a lot happened'.

Recurrent spontaneous anomalous physical events suggestive of poltergeist activity: evidence for discarnate agency?

Paul Burgess, *Journal of the Society of Psychical Research*, Vol. 76.1, No. 906, January 2012. The title of the lead article in the journal by Paul Burgess, of the Dept of Physiology in Utah School of Medicine. Found by Oliver Kamm, who has a recurrent, spontaneous and anomalous ability to spot these things.

IS A SUPER-VOLCANO JUST 390 MILES FROM LONDON ABOUT TO ERUPT?

Daily Mail, 2 January 2012. The *Daily Mail* started the new year as it meant to go on. This product of the auto-Question to Which the Answer is No generator was done so well that the fine detail looked almost hand-made. The 'just 390 miles from London', as if all locations mentioned in the *Mail* are given in this form, was a particularly realistic touch.

The spread on the *Mail* website was also marvellous, featuring four images: 1. Idyllic lakeside view (a 'hidden menace' – underneath the 'tranquil' waters sits 'a volcano that could devastate Europe'); 2. Higher view of lake, showing that it is in fact nearly circular and looks as if it is in a crater; 3. Photo of a volcano (that is comparable to 'Mount Pinatubo, which caused a 0.5C drop in global temperatures when it erupted in 1991'); 4. Map. With concentric rings.

Is this life on Venus?

Mail Online, 23 January 2012. Actually, for all we know, we could ask almost any question of this picture. 'Is this a speck of dust magnified so much that the picture is all blurry?' 'Is this a dagger I see before me?' 'Has someone gone and torn the Turin Shroud?' And the answer would still be no.

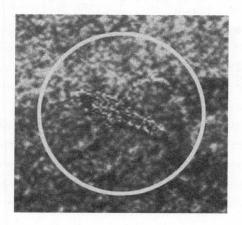

Could Spider-Man become a reality?

Daily Mail, 6 February 2012. Well, a science-obsessed student could be bitten by a radioactive spider. But he still would not be able to stick to walls or shoot web out of his hands.

Would smacking children have stopped the London riots?

The Week, 6 February 2012. 'Come out of that Foot Locker now, young man, or this passing toddler will get a slap.' No. Don't think that would have worked.

Is Tony Blair became a 'Reptilian'?

abovetopsecret.com, 9 February 2012. A question asked, in boisterous defiance of conventional grammar, on a website called abovetopsecret.com (its slogan was 'Deny Ignorance'). The writer said of a clip of Blair being interviewed by Piers Morgan at CNN: 'Noticed something strange in the look and the eyes of this man? ... I'm not a believer in "Reptilians", however, this video is really pretty odd.' I think this was a reference to David Icke, who believes that the world is ruled by two-legged lizards from the constellation Draco, inhabiting the lower levels of the fourth dimension – that is, the one closest to physical reality. Not odd at all. What is really suspicious, though, is that the *Daily Mail* failed to follow this up.

Did Hitler father a lovechild?

***Daily Mail*, 18 February 2012.** The *Daily Mail* published evidence in the form of a photograph of M Loret (below right) that shows conclusively that he and Hitler had *similar moustaches*. When you consider that the *Daily Telegraph* had the day before revealed that their handwriting looked similar, the case was a slam dunk.

Could Boris be back in the Commons by Christmas?

David Herdson, politicalbetting.com, 18 February 2012. David Herdson got a little ahead of himself at the prospect of Boris Johnson's failing to be re-elected, three months before the election for Mayor of London. His article included the golden line: 'Six events would need to take place.' The first, that he would be beaten by Ken Livingstone in May 2012, failed to occur.

DID HITLER LIVE TO OLD AGE HERE IN ARGENTINA?

Sun on Sunday, **4 March 2012**. The launch of the *Sun on Sunday* on 26 February 2012 was of great significance in the British media industry, and of no less importance to the Questions to Which the Answer is No cottage industry. In only its second edition, the *Sun on Sunday* made its debut in the series, with this question asked in the headline on a despatch from San Carlos de Bariloche.

Did the Moon sink the *Titanic*?

Daily Mail, **6 March 2012**. It was that 'supermoon' again, an inexhaustible source of Questions to Which the Answer is No. When the Moon is closer to the Earth, tides are slightly higher than usual, and headlines in the *Mail* with question marks at the end of them 'reach epidemic proportions'.

Is this the most aggressively atheistic government in Britain's history?

Alexander Boot, *Daily Mail,* **13 March 2012.** You might have thought that David Cameron had introduced a Church of England Disestablishment Bill with provisions to ban acts of worship in schools. But the article was about bans on employees wearing religious symbols at British Airways and the Royal Devon & Exeter Health Trust, bans that were being contested at the European Court of Human Rights. The connection with the coalition Government was tenuous, therefore, and the notion that it was aggressive ridiculous.

Can Mary Portas kick-start the clothing industry by manufacturing a British pair of knickers?

Channel 4 News, 14 March 2012. Mary Portas, fresh from advising the Government how to turn round high street retailing, made a television series about her reopening an underwear factory in Manchester.

ONE DIRECTION BIGGER THAN THE BEATLES?

contactmusic.com, 16 March 2012. One Direction are, apparently, a popular, but not that popular, music combination, which won a television talent competition. Well, a television competition.

Are video games just propaganda and training tools for the military?

Guardian, 18 March 2012. The top selling video game in the UK that week was *FIFA Street*, a football simulation.

WAS WINSTON CHURCHILL TO BLAME FOR TITANIC?

Sun, 26 March 2012. Churchill was President of the Board of Trade, 1908–10, responsible for shipping safety laws in the period that the *Titanic*, which sank in 1912, was being built. According to Robert Strange, 'an investigative journalist and former newspaper crime reporter', in a new book.

Did Tories spur petrol panic to avoid recession?

Sunny Hundal, liberalconspiracy.org, 29 March 2012. Sunny Hundal on the Liberal Conspiracy website suggested that, in advising people to stock up on petrol in jerry cans, Francis Maude, the Cabinet Office minister, had a Baldrick-style cunning plan.

Did MI6 agent kill spy in bag?

Daily Mail, **31 March 2012.** The story came complete with that adornment of the genre, the list of 'The Unanswered Questions'. We do not need to list them in full, but at least one of them is another Question to Which the Answer is No: 'Is it significant that an expert brought in to search for evidence of forced entry was hampered because the front door had been taken from its hinges and locks removed?'

Was Shakespeare a Jewish woman?

Jewish Book Council, 17 April 2012. This is one of the more unusual examples of the sub-genre of Questions to Which the Answer is No, questions posed by the crank industry of Shakespeare denialists.

Was murdered Briton a spy?

Daily Mail, **21 April 2012.** A different death on the front page of the *Daily Mail.* This one was about Neil Heywood, who died in China, and who had the car number plate 007. Although that might have been a fiendishly clever double bluff.

IS MY DEAD CAT OK?

Mirror, **23 April 2012.** A reader asked Psychic Sally. Fortunately, Sally was able to reassure her: 'He will always be with you; he has such a huge place in your heart.'

In the same edition of the *Mirror*: 'Is sugar worse for you than smoking?'

Are indie movies getting too pretty?

The Atlantic, **26 April 2012.** Something to do with high definition pictures.

ARE DADS THE NEW MOMS?

Wall Street Journal, **11 May 2012.** Everything wrong in just five words (one of which is 'moms'). Something is the new something else is a tired journalistic formula, but this one also manages to be sexist and trite on the basis of an old statistic, quoting a Census report which claimed that '32 per cent of fathers with working wives routinely care for their children under age 15, up from 26 per cent in 2002'.

The '90s – best decade for music ever?

NME, 11 May 2012. I am not saying it was bad, but some of us were alive in the 1960s, 1970s and 1980s. Also the 2000s and 2010s.

I'm reluctant to bring this up again, but is there a relationship between the decline of smoking (pondering things with a cigar) and the decline of profits at JP Morgan on smoke-free Wall Street?

David Hockney, *Guardian*, 14 May 2012. Asked in a letter to the editor. Bruno Michel Iksil, a trader at JP Morgan Chase, had just lost $2bn in 'poorly monitored' trades, which might have done more to explain the decline of its profits. It was not reported whether Iksil was a smoker.

Did Jesus foresee the US Constitution?

Andrew Sullivan, the *Daily Beast*, 29 May 2012. Andrew Sullivan asked this in the headline on an article about Mormonism. Possibly not a genuine Question to Which the Answer is No, unless Sullivan believes that the Reformation, the rise of capitalism and the colonisation of the New World were predicted in 1st-century Judaea.

DID LIFE ON EARTH ORIGINATE FROM ZOMBIE MICROBES?

NPR, 29 May 2012. Those are microbes that rise from under the ground singing 'Thriller' in falsetto voices, presumably. Asked by NPR, National Public Radio in the US, for whom 'zombie' seems to mean 'extra-terrestrial'.

DOES THE PENTAGON HAVE THE RIGHT WEAPONS TO FIGHT OFF AN ALIEN INVASION?

Foreign Policy **magazine, 30 May 2012.** If it is Daleks, everyone knows that conventional weapons bounce off them, because you have to have that scene where the soldiers from Unit (Unified Intelligence Taskforce) grit their teeth and shoot them with machine guns and say, 'It's useless, sir!'

Was the internet invented in 1934?

Daily Mail, **8 June 2012.** This was a question about Paul Otlet, a Belgian scientist, who wrote a book, published in 1934, which mentioned the possibility of combining television and the telephone.

Did Republicans deliberately crash the US economy?

Michael Cohen, *Guardian*, 9 June 2012. Talk about a 'vast right-wing conspiracy' – which is how Hillary Clinton denounced allegations of financial and sexual impropriety against her husband. Michael Cohen in the *Guardian* seemed to suggest that the Republican Party engineered the financial crisis in anticipation of the election of Barack Obama in November 2008. (Actually, Cohen suggested that they prolonged the economic difficulties by blocking stimulus measures in Congress. But the answer is still no.)

Baghdad spa offers fish pedicures: are luxury treatments the newest sign of progress?

***Huffington Post*, 10 June 2012.** The *Huffington Post* wondered whether Iraq might finally be set on a more hopeful course. You know that thing where you put your feet in a warm bath and tropical fish nibble the dead skin? Yes? No.

BO: POLITICAL LIABILITY?

politico.com, 14 June 2012. Asked by *Politico* about the Presidential Dog. Someone at George Washington University had done a study of political pets. A 'systematic analysis of voting behavior' and a 'voluminous library of compelling insider accounts' concluded that presidents' pets can be an asset in good times but add to unpopularity in times of economic hardship; the pets 'frolicking on the White House lawn' can enhance perceptions of inequality and make people think that 'being president is not a full-time job,' the study concluded.

Byron Tau, the *Politico* writer, later updated his report by quoting Forrest Maltzman, Professor of Political Science at George Washington University, who led the research: 'The data and conclusions are real even if there were some tongue-in-cheek references… Every now and then, we like to take our methodological skills and apply them to seemingly goofy, but still interesting, political questions.'

Is your font racist?

***Wall Street Journal*, 20 June 2012.** To do with Chinese-style lettering on an advert for Stir Fry Kits and Dumplings.

Are there any more Questions to Which the Answer is No in this book?

ACKNOWLEDGEMENTS

I am grateful to John Mullin, the editor of the *Independent on Sunday*, and my other colleagues for tolerating my interest in some of the foibles of our trade. My thanks to Olivia Bays, my editor at Elliott & Thompson, who saw the chance to turn a second of my blog themes into a book. For this one, as I hope I have already made clear, I am indebted to Oliver Kamm, now a leader-writer at *The Times*, from whom I borrowed the idea of Questions to Which the Answer is No in the first place. He has continued to contribute to the series, with a remarkable ability to find the most improbable examples. I am grateful to several other cult adherents, including Alan Beattie, International Economy Editor of the *Financial Times*, and author of the 'Immutable Law of Headlines', and all the readers who have contributed to the series over the past three years. If I had not put the word 'crowdsourced' on the Banned List, that would be how I would say that this book was put together. As it is, I can only describe it as a collaborative venture in which I am merely the record-keeper. I thank you all.

ABOUT THE AUTHOR

John Rentoul has for three years compiled what has been called 'the most useless collection of headlines' consisting of Questions to Which the Answer is No. The series has earned him a cult following on his blog and on Twitter. His book, *The Banned List* (also published by Elliott & Thompson), takes its title and subject from another blog series, in which he collects over-used, meaningless and offensive words and phrases. He is chief political commentator for the *Independent on Sunday*, and visiting fellow at Queen Mary, University of London, where he teaches contemporary history. Previously he has worked for the BBC and *New Statesman*, and on farms in Canada, where he picked tobacco.

QUESTION SOURCES

PRINTED AND ONLINE NEWSPAPERS AND MAGAZINES

The Atlantic
Christian Today
City AM
Daily Express
Daily Mail
Daily Mirror
Daily Telegraph
The Economist
Evening Standard
Financial Times
Foreign Policy
Guardian
History Today
Huffington Post
Independent
Le Monde
London Evening Standard
Mail Online
Mail on Sunday
New Republic
New York Times
New Scientist
New Statesman
NME
PC Magazine
The New Yorker
Observer
Politico
Progress
Salem News
The Spectator
Sun on Sunday
Sun
Sunday Telegraph
Time
The Times
Total Politics
TV Guide
Vanity Fair
Wall Street Journal
The Week

JOURNALS

Biblical Archeology Review
Journal of the Society of Psychical Research
Psychological Science
Mineral Products Today

BLOGS

UK Forces Media Ops team blog
Clive Soley's blog
Coffee House blog
Conservative Home
Dale & Co. blog
Guardian Science blog
Harry's Place
Hopi Sen's blog
Iain Dale's blog
Iain Martin's blog
Independent blog
Keep Tony For PM
Left Foot Forward
Liberal Conspiracy
Marbury
Not Exactly Rocket Science
Peter Kenyon's blog
Sky News blog
Telegraph blog
Telegraph Film blog
The Daily Censored
Times blog

WEBSITES

Abovetopsecret
BBC News
Bloomberg
Business Green
Catch the Fire Ministries
Contactmusic
Examiner
GigaOM
Healthcare Republic
International Economics
Investors.com
Iraq Inquiry Digest

KashmirWatch
Michael K. Reynolds
Newser
OurKingdom
Peter Kellner
Political Betting
The Big Peace
The Daily Beast
The Score
Ynetnews

TV

BBC4
BBC News report
BBC Northern Ireland
Channel 4 News
Discovery Channel

Fox 26 News, Houston
Fox News
Sky News

BOOKS

The Real Global Warming Disaster by
    Christopher Booker (Continuum, 2011)

OTHER SOURCES

UKIP
NPR, National Public Radio in the US
Jewish Book Council
Manchester United supporters internet
    forum
Socialist Workers Party meeting poster
Soil Association
Speakers Forum at Glastonbury

PICTURE CREDITS

Page 124: From US Patent Application 20110194230 by Gregory M. Hart et al., 11 August 2011

Page 126: Public domain, via Wikimedia Commons

Page 131: © NASA

Page 135: Image by Leonid Ksanfomaliti, first published in *Solar System Research*, Vol. 45, No. 7, 2011

Page 137: (left) Getty Images; (right) Photograph of M Loret first published in *Le Point*, Paris, 17 February 2012, by François Gibault

Page 138: By NASA/JPL/USGS (NASA Image of the Day) [Public domain], via Wikimedia Commons

Page 141: © *Daily Mail*, 31 March 2012

Page 142: In Helmolt, H.F., ed. *History of the World*. New York: Dodd, Mead and Company, 1902. Author unknown [Public domain or Public domain], via Wikimedia Commons

INDEX OF QUESTIONS/HEADLINES